SOUTH AFRICA OF TO-DAY

SOUTH AFRICA OF TO-DAY

BY

CAPTAIN FRANCIS YOUNGHUSBAND, C.I.E.

INDIAN STAFF CORPS
LATE SPECIAL CORRESPONDENT OF "THE TIMES" IN SOUTH AFRICA, GOLD MEDALLIST, ROYAL GEOGRAPHICAL SOCIETY, AUTHOR OF "THE HEART OF A CONTINENT" AND "THE RELIEF OF CHITRAL"

WITH ILLUSTRATIONS

GYAN

Published by

Gyan Publishing House
5, Ansari Road
Daryaganj, New Delhi-110002
Phone: 011-47034999, 9811692060
E-mail: books@gyanbooks.com

Distribution Network
gyanbooks.com
India, USA, Canada, UK, Australia, France

ISBN : 978-81-212-4045-1 (PB)
First Published, 1898

2nd Impression 2020

Printed at: Gyan Press, Delhi.

South Africa of To-Day
Author: Captain Francis Younghusband

PREFACE

I AM indebted to the management of *The Times* for their permission to republish the letters and telegrams addressed to them during my two missions to South Africa; and I would wish to take this opportunity of recording my appreciation of the support invariably afforded me in carrying out the duty with which they had intrusted me.

F. E. YOUNGHUSBAND

October, 1897

CONTENTS

LIST OF ILLUSTRATIONS

SOUTH AFRICA OF TO-DAY

CHAPTER I

INTRODUCTION

AFTER more than twelve years of wandering in India, China, and Central Asia, and after having but very recently returned from the Chitral campaign on the Indian frontier, I had expected to have passed in England some little of the two years' leave of absence to which I had for so long been looking forward. But trouble was brewing in South Africa, and when the *Times* asked me to go out to the Cape in their interest, I could not resist the temptation of accepting the invitation.

My only qualification for the work must have been that I knew absolutely nothing about it My old regiment, the King's Dragoon Guards, had taken part in the Zulu war, and afterwards formed a portion of the garrison of the Transvaal; so, from conversation at the mess table, I had gathered some hazy ideas of places in it, and I had in my mind some crude and disconnected scraps of information regarding its recent history—the Boer war, the discovery of gold in the

Transvaal, the rise of the Chartered Company, and the Matabele campaign. But on all essential points in the political situation, and even the geography, I was as ignorant as South Africans would be of the Indian frontier. I had only this advantage, that for the last ten years almost my sole occupation in life had been travelling in little known countries and reporting what I saw and heard there. So as soon as I had put the last remaining touches on my book of travels then about to be published, I eagerly read up the works on South African history and travel which I had brought on board for the purpose of forming in my mind a groundwork on which to build.

On my arrival in Cape Town, in the beginning of December, I found the situation in the Transvaal was fast reaching a crisis. Mr. Lionel Phillips, the President of the Chamber of Mines at Johannesburg, had but recently made a speech in which he detailed the disabilities under which the huge gold-mining industry laboured, and hinted in strong terms that, were concessions of some sort not granted by the Boer Government, the Uitlanders (or foreign residents) might be compelled to resort to force to gain their ends; and everywhere people were saying that trouble was pending.

But I stayed for a few days only in Cape Town, and then hurried on to Johannesburg. A long tedious railway journey of three nights and two days brought me at last to this remarkable town, of which I found I had previously formed no accurate conception.

For two days we had been passing over first the weird and desolate KARROO, and then the limitless prairies of the Orange Free State. Occasionally a solitary farmhouse would be seen, but seldom anything approaching in size to a village; and only one small town—Bloemfontein—was passed in the whole distance from Cape Town to Johannesburg. At last, on the morning of the third day, springing suddenly out of the same rolling prairies as before, we saw tall iron chimneys, the lofty headgears and corrugated iron buildings of mines; and now we were close upon the GOLDEN CITY. The train crawled on, we rolled into a maze of corrugated iron shanties of every shape and size and divided into square blocks by long straight dusty roads, and we had arrived in Johannesburg, the scene of the revolution that was to be.

Those who are acquainted with the towns in the Western States of America can probably form an idea of what sort of place Johannesburg is. But never having visited the United States or any newly-formed colony, I was astonished at the extremes it presented in every particular except one. There was squalor and luxury; there was dirt outside and cleanliness within; there were funny little shanties built of biscuit tins nailed together, and there were palatial business offices and private residences; there were low dirty stores and shops which would not be out of place in Regent Street; there were black men and white; eager busy men and listless loafers. In everything else there was contrast; but there was no contrast to the new; there was no old—not even old men. The whole town had been in existence for less than a dozen years, and whatever there was had been collected and constructed in that time. Here it was, with a population of 50,000 whites and 50,000 blacks—all keen, energetic, pushing—except those few who had already been crushed under in the struggle for wealth. And this was the town I had come 6,000 miles by water and 1,000 miles by land to see, and which was now on the brink of a revolution.

That with a pushing, enterprising population like this at Johannesburg, yearly increasing in numbers and yearly feeling more acutely the weight of the heavy Boer Government on the top of them, a revolution must some day take place if an outlet were not given to their outflowing energy, had for many years been recognised.

As far back as 1890, Sir Charles Dilke, in his *Problems of Greater Britain*, ventured to foretell that before half-a-dozen years should pass President Kruger would either have to grant concessions or face a revolution.

Nor is it any secret that successive British Governments, Liberal as well as Conservative, had felt it necessary to consider such an eventuality and the steps it would necessitate to prevent a general

COMMISSIONER STREET, JOHANNESBURG.

[To face page 4.

disturbance to the peace of South Africa. Now, therefore, when they were on the verge of a crisis, I eagerly sought out those who could inform me best upon the situation.

In Johannesburg there is considerable difficulty in arriving at the truth upon any given point, but there is no difficulty whatever in getting a man to express the views which he individually holds for the time being upon any question; and by a process of balancing one is enabled to arrive approximately at the spot where the centre of gravity really stands. Such men as Charles Leonard and Lionel Phillips—the one the chairman of the political organisation known as the Transvaal National Union, and the other the chairman of the Johannesburg Chamber of Mines—were of course at that time most pronounced in their views upon the situation; and if opinions differed as to the means which should be taken to secure a redress of the grievances which the Uitlander population held against the Boer Government there was a universal opinion that legitimate grievances did exist. It was very generally felt that the ignorant, slow-moving Government of the Boers was not precisely the one best adapted for the guidance and control of an intelligent and enterprising mining population, and that until the Government could be made to move faster and conform more fully to the spirit of the majority of the population it controlled, the mining industry could not prosper to the extent which might be expected from the richness of the country. And these material resources of the Transvaal being the basis upon which the whole fabric of its prosperity rests, and upon which all calculation as to its future development depends, I will first set forth, as reliably as I was able to obtain them, the details on it. It was the gold which attracted the Uitlander population to the Transvaal. It is the gold which they extract that furnishes yearly the revenue of five millions to the former pauper government of the Boers. And it is the gold and other mineral resources which will keep the population there and attract more men to the Transvaal. If the gold is likely to "pinch out," and if there prove to be no other mineral resources in the country, there would scarcely be sufficient reason to resort to revolutions in order to improve the method of government. But if, as will be shown, there is, to a certainty, hundreds of millions of pounds sterling of gold hidden in the Transvaal, and with such facilities in regard to climate, water supply, and labour as make the obtaining of that gold perfectly feasible; if besides the gold there prove to be vast quantities of coal and iron in juxtaposition, besides many and other lesser minerals; and if, in addition, there are fair agricultural possibilities;—then those who are engaged in developing these vast resources might be expected to demand that the government of the country should treat their efforts with sympathy and encouragement; and European nations who have to look out now for suitable fields of emigration for their surplus population must be interested in seeing that one of the fairest still remaining is not ruined and wasted through maladministration.

CHAPTER II

RESOURCES OF THE TRANSVAAL

OF the suitability of the climate of the Transvaal to European colonisation the experience of the Boers gives ample proof. On the vast rolling plains of the high veldt situated at an elevation of from 4,000 to 5,000 feet above sea-level, the climate is very similar to that of Southern Europe, though neither quite so hot in summer nor so cold in winter as the climate of Italy. The heat of summer is tempered by rain, and the winter is dry and sunny. That the climate is altogether so productive of energy as that of Europe is, I think, open to doubt. The rarity of the atmosphere, due to the height above sea-level, the extreme dryness, and the incessant staring sunshine, may perhaps be found to conduce toward a certain listlessness and laziness of character. Still, the Boers, who have been born and bred here, and who belong to families which have been settled in South Africa for a couple of centuries, are as strong and robust as the average European. It may therefore be taken as an established fact that the climate of the Transvaal, exclusive of the low-lying districts, is well adapted to European colonisation; and on the highlands of the country there is room for two or three millions of settlers.

In regard to the mineral resources of the country the marvellous production of gold of which it is capable is well known. Last year the Transvaal produced gold to the value of eight and-a-half millions—about one-fifth of the total production of gold in the world, and equalling the production of the United States and Australia respectively. Moreover, the amount of annual production increases year by year. Since 1890 it has increased at the rate of £1,200,000 a year, and, with the number of new stamps being put up, it has been calculated that with good administration £26,000,000 annually might be produced, and that within fifty years £700,000,000, of which £200,000,000 will be clear profit, will have been taken from the Rand mines alone. These are the calculations of experienced mining engineers, based on the results actually obtained by mining companies. And even these estimates are considered too low by so great an authority as Mr. Hays Hammond, He points out that in many instances the lives of mines increase as exploitation proceeds; that, as the economic conditions of mining become more favourable, as the mines are worked upon a larger scale and with better management, lower-grade ores may be more profitably mined; and that payable reefs will almost certainly be found in outside districts. In this unique country all the conditions favourable to successful gold mining seem to be combined. The remarkable regularity of the gold deposits render possible the nicest calculations as to the whereabouts and amount of the gold, so that there is little speculation but a practical certainty as to the profits. The existence of an inexhaustible coal field directly in connection with the gold deposits furnishes a plentiful, cheap, and easily-obtained fuel supply. Water in sufficient quantity is obtainable. The climate is good. Native labour can be procured. And lastly, owing to the ore deposits being in one continuous stretch, a concentration of energy in the development of the mines is made possible, and considerable economy is thereby effected. In these circumstances, the gold-mining industry may be expected to flourish for many years to come. For exactly how many years it would not be possible to say, for the life of a mine depends upon the cost of working it; upon the rapidity with which it is worked; upon the number of stamps employed; upon new methods which may make it possible to wash low-grade ores; and upon whether one or more levels are worked at the same time. But it would probably be a safe forecast to say that fifty years hence the gold resources of the Transvaal will not have been exhausted.

But when, sixty, seventy, or a hundred years hence, the gold has all been cleared out of the country, is there no industry which may take the place of the gold mining? Fortunately there is. The existence of coal has already been alluded to, and besides this there are vast quantities of iron ore of a quality better than that obtained in England, and immediately adjoining yet other coal beds furnishing good coking coal; and silver, copper, lead, and other minerals are found in various parts of the country.

To deal with the coal first. In one colliery, not half-a-dozen miles from the gold mines, I have seen a seam of coal 70ft. in thickness. This coal, though of low quality, suffices for the purposes of the gold mines, and there is a sufficient quantity of it to outlast far the lives of all the gold mines.

Besides these coal deposits near the gold fields and those others by the Vaal river, which furnish coal for the railway system far down into the Cape Colony, there are literally hundreds, perhaps even a thousand square miles of coal in the Middelberg and Ermelo districts lying between Pretoria and Delagoa Bay. In the midst of these coal beds is the outcrop of iron ore. And running through them is the lately-constructed railway to Delagoa Bay. With these vast coal fields close to a first-rate port on the Indian Ocean, the prospects of the coal-mining industry seem brilliant. The great fleets of ocean-going steamers which run to

India, Australia, and China, and to South and East Africa, at present draw their coal supplies for the most part from England. But if the Transvaal coal proved suitable in quality they would draw much of their coal from this country. More than one of the great steamship lines have already sent representatives to the Transvaal to make inquiries and inspect. And it is with a view to supplying this great market that the mineral rights on the land have been acquired by syndicates of the various great financial houses in the Transvaal, and mining operations pushed rapidly forward. I have visited mine after mine along the line of railway. Few of these are more than a year old, while most have only been started for a few months. And besides these already existing mines, others are being planned out at the most advantageous positions by the railway.

While there is thus an amount of coal which the State mining engineer, in his last annual report, describes as "inexhaustible for an indefinite period," and the quantity is assured, the quality has yet to be practically proved; and it is upon the quality that depends the question whether the fast steamship lines and men-of-war will use it or not. First-class vessels, with their delicately-adjusted boiler and furnace arrangements, and with limited carrying space, cannot afford to use any but the best coal, and Transvaal coal may not suit them. The best coal has not yet been put on the market. The industry is only in its infancy. Most of the mines are outcrop mines, and outcropping coal is seldom so good as that found further in. The best analysis I have seen—an analysis showing a percentage of ash of only 5·4—was of coal from a spot six miles from the railway, and this coal will not be worked till a siding from the railway is made. Again, in the Ermelo district there is said to be coal little inferior to Cardiff coal, but this cannot be put on the market till the projected branch line from that district is completed. Until, therefore, the mining companies have exploited their best coal, until branch lines and sidings have been constructed to enable their best coal to be put on the market, and until this coal has been practically tested on the steamers, no estimate as to the extent to which it will be used can be formed. But that faith is placed in the future of this coal industry is shown by the fact that every leading financial house—without, I think, an exception—has lately acquired coal properties. Even if the coal does not prove good enough for use on the fastest-steaming men-of-war and ocean liners, it may be used by minor steamship lines and cargo vessels, many of which already use it. And in view of the development in railway communication and the consequent reduction in rates, and to the improvement which may be expected in the present rough methods of handling the coal at the pit's mouth, on the railway, and at Delagoa Bay, and the resulting cheapening of the cost of delivery, the prediction of a well-known pioneer of South African enterprise, that in ten years time not a ton of English coal will come to South Africa, may not improbably prove true.

Nor is it only on gold mines, steamship lines and railways that the coal will be used. There are also prospects of a great iron industry arising which would require supplies of the good coking coal which has recently been discovered and tested. Why, when the existence of a reef of magnetite from 20 to 40 feet wide, extending for several miles close alongside the coal, and of such quality as to yield 70 per cent. of metallic iron, was well known, no proper attempt has yet been made to start an iron industry will seem strange. The reasons are that till two years ago there was no railway through the iron district, that good coking coal had not been discovered, that the expense of importing coke from England was almost prohibitive, and that the cost of both white and coloured labour has hitherto been excessive. The existence of one of those curses of this country, a concession, set a still further bar upon enterprise in this direction. Now, however, that the railway has been made, that coking coal has been found close to the iron, that wages of the natives are in process of reduction, and white labour has become plentiful, efforts are being made to start an iron industry. And if the prophecy of a Durham engineer, that the time would come when even the railway engines would be made in this country from materials obtained on the spot, may be held as applying to too distant a period for present consideration, yet no one who has been round the great stores of mining requirements in Johannesburg and seen the quantities of pig iron, bar iron, sheet iron, light rails, &c., kept there, and has learned that iron which costs from 40*s.* to 45*s.* in England costs £12 out here, can help thinking that at any rate these simple necessaries of the mines might be furnished from the country itself, or that all such ironwork as only requires casting, such as the great supports for machinery and iron trucks used on the mines, might with advantage be made here, instead of being imported. A glance from the railway train shows a variety of objects which might well be made of iron obtained in the country. The great headgears of the mines, now made of timber, costing 4*s.* 6*d.* to 5*s.* per cubic foot, and imported from such distant countries as British Columbia, would be made of iron if iron were available. Johannesburg is, one might almost say, built of corrugated iron, and among all the thousands of houses there I have seen only one which had not a corrugated iron roof. Even the houses of the Boers are now being roofed with this material instead of thatch. Might not all the corrugated iron required in the little townships now everywhere springing up in the vicinity of the coal and gold mines be manufactured here? Might not iron sleepers, rails, iron telegraph posts, lamp posts, and many other things of simple manufacture and requiring little less than casting or rolling, be turned out in this country?

Men of practical experience believe that they may. The gold mining has so far absorbed all the interest, but it can scarcely be doubted that an iron industry will soon be started. Iron may be exported to India, Australia, and even America. And long after the gold mines have been made as empty as the craters of the moon the iron industry will be flourishing in the Transvaal.

Of the other minerals obtained in the Transvaal little need be said, and it only remains to consider the agricultural resources. On first looking at the plentiful foliage in Johannesburg—seven-year-old trees often 40 feet in height—and on seeing evidences of the rapidity of growth of varied kinds of vegetable produce, one is tempted to believe that the agricultural prospects of the country may be as brilliant as the mineral. But the experiences of those who have tried farming have not hitherto been very encouraging. Trees certainly grow well, because there is plenty of water under the soil, and because their roots can readily penetrate to a great depth. But the soil where these surprising results in tree-growing have been obtained is not really rich, and has little staying power unless manure be applied. And agriculture has many natural obstacles to contend with. Hailstorms of unexampled severity occur every three years or so, beating down the crops and destroying the fruit. Last year locusts ate up the crops and the leaves of the fruit trees. It is said that wheat cannot be grown in summer because the rain falls in that season and causes rust, and in winter there is all sun and no rain, so that to grow wheat irrigation must be resorted to. Again, the cost of labour is almost prohibitive, for the mines give very high wages. With all these drawbacks agriculture cannot be said now to flourish in the Transvaal. Still much may be done in timber growing, and by selecting rust-proof varieties of wheat which could grow in summer, by choosing thick-skinned fruits which could resist the hail, especially if they are left on the tree only to the stage when they may be plucked to ripen indoors. And, again, by the introduction of every kind of labour-saving machinery on the farms, and by the construction of irrigation works, agriculturists hope to make agriculture successful. When many of the hotels still give tinned butter on the table, when condensed tinned milk is half the price of fresh milk, and when nearly the whole of the wheat is imported from Australia and other countries, it will easily be recognised that there is scope for agricultural development in this country. On the great expanse of grass-covered veldt vast numbers of cattle and sheep might find support, and such necessaries of life as meat and milk and butter be provided. In the variety of soil and climate which is found in this country place may yet be found where either tea, or coffee, or sugar may be grown as successfully as tobacco now is. Few, I think, will imagine that this country will ever export wool, or wheat, or coffee, or any other agricultural product.

But there is every reason to believe that all the ordinary food necessaries may be grown in the country in sufficient abundance to supply the needs of its population.

From all that has been said about the climate and the mineral and agricultural resources of the country we may, I think, draw the following conclusions :—

(1) That immigration into the Transvaal will steadily increase.

(2) That the greater portion of the incoming population is likely to remain permanently.

(3) That this population will be a wealthy population.

The importance of these fundamental factors in the consideration of the future of the country will be evident when we come to discuss the character and relative positions of the various groups of which the population is composed.

CHAPTER III

THE BOERS

THIS country of the Transvaal, which is approximately the same size as Great Britain and Ireland, somewhat larger than Italy, and but little smaller than Prussia, and which is, as we have just seen, admirably adapted for colonisation, abounding in gold and in addition possessing a practically inexhaustible supply of coal and all the possibilities of a great iron industry, is at present inhabited by a black population of about three-quarters of a million (the approximate population of Calcutta) and by a white population of a quarter of a million (about the same as that of Bristol). Yet it is actually governed by a small minority of even the white inhabitants; and the President of the South African Republic has at his back to support him in controlling and developing the country a number of subjects which would be exceeded by such provincial towns as York or small counties as Westmorland. The Boers of the Transvaal number no more than 70,000 or 80,000; yet they rule twice that number of white aliens, and ten times that number of black inhabitants: and, as the future of the country must in a large degree depend upon the character of the people who rule it, I will devote this chapter to a consideration of the leading characteristics of these Boer rulers of the Transvaal.

The story of how—some in the pure colonising spirit and some to avoid religious persecution—a party of several hundred of Dutchmen and French Huguenots came to settle at the Cape of Good Hope with their wives and families is now well known. These men were of the same blood as those who had withstood the great power of Philip of Spain, and were prepared to risk life itself rather than forgo any portion of their liberty. Arriving at the Cape towards the end of the seventeenth century, the two nationalities of which the emigrant band was composed quickly mingled together through inter-marriage and the cruel suppression of the French language, and they further mixed with a set of rough adventurers already planted there under the Dutch East India Company then governing the colony.

At this starting point of their South African history, the Boers may be said to have possessed three leading characteristics—courage, a profound love of independence, and strong religious convictions. They were men of hard resolute natures, who sought in the new world a refuge from the restraints of the old. From that starting point we have to watch the influence of their new surroundings acting on their character, strengthening it in one direction, and sapping into it in another. We have to note their struggles with men, developing their courage and military qualities, and increasing, if possible, their resolution to be independent; and to mark how the lavishness of nature in these favoured southern lands inclined them to indolence and ease; while through all we shall see how their religion has supported them in their trials, and preserved them from that rapid degradation of character which has befallen other peoples in similar circumstances.

Two centuries ago, when the original emigrants landed at the Cape, the fear of attacks from natives was so great and the country was so overrun with lions and other wild animals, that no white man lived further than forty-five miles from the castle at Cape Town. To guard against attack every man was made liable to military service, and all were required to meet for drill and practice in the use of arms. So from the first the Boer acquired a training in military duties; and became accustomed to the idea of, in his own person, defending his liberty. And this habit was confirmed as he gradually began to feel his feet and set off on long wanderings into the interior of Africa.

At first the colonists had contented themselves with simply cultivating the land near Cape Town and leading a purely agricultural existence; but partly through a need of cattle, partly from a spirit of adventure, and partly because of the oppressive conduct of the Dutch officials at Cape Town, numbers of them were led to seek, on the uplands of the interior, pasture-land where cattle might be bred and where they themselves might be free from the irksome restraints and petty tyrannies of the settled districts. The peasant farmer laboriously tilling his fields from year to year was now transformed into the roving, dreamy herdsman. The agricultural was given up for the pastoral life, the cottage for the waggon, civilisation for nature, and the Boer might wander whither he would. The only direct tax he had to pay was at the rate of 1*d.* a year for five acres. He had slaves to tend his cattle and do his hard work for him. And his career would have been smooth and easy but for one consideration—he had to carry on incessant struggle with his fellow men. The land was not to be had for the asking. There were native tribes who had claims over it, and these had to be fought. The Boer had much to thank Nature for. She had made it possible for him to live with the minimum of exertion; and he thoroughly appreciated her consideration in that respect, and exerted himself as little as need be. He never troubled himself about education. He made no efforts to enrich himself by industry or care, and no ambitions were allowed to consume his soul. He simply partook of the ample food which nature so easily provided, and lived on day by day and year by year in unvarying monotony. But man was ever against him. The Boer was never free from the attacks of the stealthy Bushman. He could never feel safe from the raids of the Kafirs. And so, while on the one hand all was tending to a peaceful, easy existence, on the other a strenuous life of constant watchfulness was required.

A century rolled away while the Boers spread themselves over the interior of the colony, and then the rule passed from the hands of the Dutch into the hands of the English, and the Boers became British subjects. They had not found government even by their own countrymen at the Cape congenial to them, and had twice revolted against even the Dutch government. So, as they gradually became aware that there were rich pasture lands away to the north beyond the limits of Cape Colony, it is not surprising that they wandered away in search of this new country, and to free themselves from the control of their new rulers. In 1836, thousands of them joined in the "Great Trek," and with their wives and their families, their flocks and their herds, crossed the Orange river and made their way to the Transvaal and Natal. It was the commencement of that hardest struggle of all in their history, which has lasted up to the present year, and left such marks that of the twenty-four members of the present Volksraad, seventeen bear bullet wounds, while there is hardly a Boer family in which some female relative has not been either wounded in action or murdered by natives. After suffering horrible massacres at the hands of the Zulus, and after most bloody battles, in which even their women took part, they defeated the great Zulu chief Dingan; they cleared the Free State and the Transvaal, and set up a Republic of their own.

At last they were free. They were far away from all civilisation, and possessed of a country where each one might have his thousands of acres of grazing land, and could set up his home without any risk of seeing even the smoke of a single other house from his doorstep. What more could the Boers wish for? Yet now was the time when the weaknesses of their character became most apparent. In adversity the Boers have always been strong; in prosperity weak. They loved independence, but they hated taxation; and now that they had to tax themselves in order to carry on their own government, revenue was not forthcoming sufficient for the purpose. Nor could the Boers find adequately educated men to fill the public offices, and Government posts were held by men who could hardly write an ordinary letter. Disorder naturally followed. At one time there were four separate Republics in the Transvaal, and there were even fights between the rival factions. A man of education was imported from the Cape Colony to preside over them, and for a time matters improved; but gradually the whole administrative machinery broke down, till there was no money left in the exchequer,

Meeting of Boers at the Monument of Independence, Krugersdorf.

[To face page 25.

a native rebellion threatened the country; and, to save the peace of South Africa, the British Government stepped in and assumed the control of affairs.

But as soon as their independence was threatened back the Boers came together again. Once more their old spirit flamed up; and four years later, in 1880, on the anniversary of their victory over the great Dingan, they declared their independence, each man as he threw a stone on the cairn at Krugersdorp swearing that, if necessary, he would sacrifice his life to attain freedom for his people. Their efforts were successful, and their liberty was restored to them. Subsequently gold was discovered in the country; and now, no longer dependent on themselves alone to provide the revenue necessary for government, they were enabled to hire educated men from Europe to carry on the routine of the public offices; and the country flourished, till again, at the beginning of last year, their independence was threatened, and once more as of old they combine to resist the danger.

Now, what do we gather from this history in regard to the character of the Boers? When in face of such odds they have fought for, obtained, and kept their independence, may we not call them a courageous people? Grant that their form of courage is not such that they would seek out fighting for fighting's sake; grant that they have no special liking for advancing into the open in a battle and exposing themselves to every kind of danger, and yet they may still be a brave people; for here we see them to-day, a nation of farmer soldiers, who have never been paid to fight, but who, for two centuries in South Africa, against black man and against white, have carried on the struggle; and their courage and military capacity must surely be acknowledged and their love of independence and sturdy self-reliance established.

And what effect have the natural surroundings of South Africa had upon them? For two hundred years the Boer has lived upon the unbounded plains of South Africa till his nature has opened out like them. On his solitary farm, with the vast plain before him unbroken by a single tree or human habitation, the bright unclouded sky above, the blue hazy hills in the distance, and a soft dreamy atmosphere overshrouding all, the nature of the Boer must expand itself to the surroundings, grow more and more intolerant of restraint and less inclined to effort. There must be something peculiarly fascinating to the Boer in being able to live a perpetual out-of-door existence; to have at hand natives who in return for his allowing them a few acres to cultivate for themselves will till enough ground to supply him with all his wants, and to have no one by to vex him with competition—all this must have to the Boer a peculiar charm, and the man who lives under such conditions must often look with contempt upon him who sits in an office and frets himself on the expenditure of every sixpence in his fever to gain money. But such a life, with all its enjoyment, inevitably tends to laziness. And so we find the present-day Boer with these ruling characteristics of indolence and impatience of control indubitably marked upon him.

And, besides the natural surroundings and the struggle with man, there has been the influence of religion always working strongly on him. The strictly family life which the Boers have always led has been one great cause of their preserving this influence, and they have retained much of the Puritanism of Cromwell's time. They set out on the march, and they went into battle with no songs or jests, but in all seriousness, saying their prayers and singing hymns, with the absolute faith of Israel of old that the Lord was with them. And so deeply do their religious convictions affect their practical, every-day life that even to the present time they think it impious to take preventive measures against such plagues as locusts, considering them as a punishment sent by God. But while they fear to do anything against what they believe to be the will of God, they refuse to take credit for anything praiseworthy that they themselves accomplish. The victory over the Zulu Dingan, their successes in 1881 and last year, were ascribed to God, and not to their own prowess. The hardy Boer farmer rode from his home to defend the independence of his country with the firm conviction that God was on his side; and he returned from victory with no undue exaltation, but with that conviction more surely fixed upon him than ever.

Yet, with all this religious feeling which has preserved much of their character to them, the Boers have certainly defects which most men do not expect to find in so religious a people. It may have been due to their daily contact as children with Kafir children upon their farms, and to their continual intercourse with none but barbarous races; but it cannot be denied that much of the truthfulness and openness of character of their ancestors has been lost, and neither veracity nor honesty can be reckoned among the virtues of the Boers.

In his domestic life the Boer is generally moral, and he is strong in his family affections. Wherever he has gone he has taken his family with him. He marries early, and his wife has much to say in the husband's affairs. It is said to have been a woman who inspired the attack upon Majuba Hill. The parents are fond of their children, and the children of their parents. They are genial in their intercourse, hospitable, and fond of visiting one another. And this domestic life has done much to soften their natures. In so slow-moving a people there must be some remnants of the cruel natures of seventeenth-century men, and isolated cases of cruelty occur even now. Nor do the Boers ever forget an injury. But they are not intemperate in their vindictiveness. As a people they may be considered mild-natured, and they petitioned for mercy to be shown directly they heard of the death sentences passed upon the Reform leaders, even though they believed these leaders to have plotted against their cherished independence.

One characteristic alone remains to be noted. In their South African history they have had to wage incessant warfare with natives; and it may generally be noted that those who have had the actual carrying on of warlike operations against barbarous tribes among whom they dwell are least inclined to treat these tribes with liberality. If the present settlers in Matabeleland, for instance, had the ordering of their affairs it would be many long years before they would think of granting the natives the franchise.

Similarly the Boers, who time after time have had to fight the natives as Rhodesian settlers are now fighting the Matabele, and often to see their women and children massacred, are unable to understand people like the English, who treat natives as free men. To the Boer the black man is the hewer of wood and drawer of water. And in his attitude towards the native races of South Africa the Boer is rigidly severe, and, according to English ideas, oppressive.

Summing up, then, the characteristics of the Boers, we may call them excellent pioneers, with marvellous powers of physical endurance; a brave, self-reliant people, with high military aptitude; peace loving, yet ever ready to defend their independence; slow to move, but bitter and obstinate when roused; suspicious, but credulous, and sensitive to ridicule and criticism; genial, hospitable, and affectionate in their family relationships; a large-hearted people, and, as a result of their stern life, possessed of a broad common sense not always attained by more highly-educated nations; yet at the same time a people who, from their tendency to shirk the competition of modern life and from the effect of their surroundings, have become indolent and devoid of any ambition beyond independence, deficient in honesty and veracity, ignorant, unprogressive, and in most important respects two centuries behind other European nations.

Such are the people who control the destinies of the most promising new country in the world.

CHAPTER IV

THE BOER SYSTEM OF GOVERNMENT

This leading characteristic of the Boers being determined, and the nature of their surroundings being known, it is possible to form some conception of the State into which they have formed themselves.

One of the chief features in the Boer character, we saw, was their impatience of control; and a pastoral and nomadic people of such a character, sparsely distributed over an open country, with no natural barriers, as seas or mountains, to prevent their escape to other countries near by, would naturally tend to split up; they would have little cohesion, and would gradually separate into a number of small communities with but slight connection among them. This is, in fact, what was actually taking place among the Boers before the British annexation twenty years ago; and the treks to Bechuanaland, Mashonaland, and Portuguese territory ever since then give evidence of the same tendency. But what more than anything else has united the Boers as they are to-day has been war. Divided and scattered in peace time, they have united whenever their independence has been threatened; and pressure from outside has thus been the chief cause of their present union.

And, besides this external influence, there are certain internal influences which work towards the same end. The Boers are few in numbers, they are nearly all related to one another, and they are strong in their family affections, and generally disposed to preserve family ties; while the openness of the country, which might in certain circumstances tend to disintegration, under present conditions, by the facilities it affords for intercommunication, likewise assists in bringing about a union of the people.

In the struggle for existence among the States of South Africa the Boers have survived, then, mainly because of their capacity for military co-operation; because every man among them fought—members of their Parliament, judges of their law courts, everybody—and because the women who could not fight helped the men who could. The Boers thus became a nation of soldiers. The army was the whole people, and the whole people were an army. And whereas many of the most important acts in their history have been the results of assemblies for warlike purposes (their very Constitution having been framed at a war council by men with arms in their hands), it has come about that military and political authority have often been combined. The military gathering has been the political gathering, and the successful military leader the head of the State. The first President was a man who had led the people in many a fight. And the present chief of the State was formerly Commandant-General, and was also one of the triumvirate who conducted the War of Independence of 1880. He has been President ever since then, and his nearly successful opponent at the last elections was the present Commandant-General, who had also been one of the triumvirate in 1880.

The influence of the Church, appealing so strongly as it does among the Boers to obedience to the commands of God, strengthened the principle of subordination. And this subordination, brought about partly by religious influence, but chiefly by constant calls to arms, has been the principal factor in checking an undue amount of individual independence which the nature of the people and the character of their surroundings might have produced.

What, then, has been the resulting form of government? It might have been expected that the chronic state of war would have produced a despotism, with the people subordinated to a chief as an army to its general. And from the nature of the Boer society with its family groupings there might also be expected a tendency to despotism in the patriarchal form. President Kruger is, indeed, very fond of treating the people, and especially aliens, as children, and his language to the latter is particularly paternal. But these tendencies to despotism in the military or patriarchal form have not been sufficiently potent to override that other feature in the Boer character of which notice has been taken—his passion for individual freedom. While war has kept the Boers in subordination, when war ceases the tendency is to relax this subordination. Many instances might be quoted in which Boers have declared themselves opposed to the Government; but, on hearing that their country was attacked, have sunk their opposition and subordinated themselves strictly to the orders of their chosen leader. Yet the history of the Boers shows that during peace they demand great freedom of action, and the less frequently they are summoned to war the less they submit to the despotic control necessary in war time. As the country became more quiet the first President, a military leader, was replaced by a clergyman; and even now not only the Commandant-General but every commandant under him is elected by the people. These democratic tendencies are given further play because neither has there been time, nor is the temper of the people suited, for the formation of any distinct social classes. The Boers have had in their time to do much fighting; but not being really warlike, but on the contrary peace-loving, they have had no inclination to form a class of hereditary nobles or military leaders. They have all alike been exposed to the same influences. Not a part of them only but all of them have had to fight.

They have all alike up till now led the same semi-agricultural, semi-pastoral existence. None have taken to mining, nor is there any trading instinct in them. And as there is no sea-coast there is no temptation for any to adopt a seafaring life. The consequence is that the Boers have remained a homogeneous people, with no distinction of classes among them. There is little accumulation of wealth, and no inclination to form a separate class on account of wealth. There are no families distinctly above the rest, and no tendency to form an hereditary leadership. Every man has, therefore, an equal chance of coming to the front. And the rigidity of social structure which might have followed, and which religious influences foster, has so far been avoided, and, in this respect, at any rate, the Boer people do not present an obstacle to progress.

The resulting Constitution, as might have been expected, is one partially despotic and partially democratic—a republic in name, but a republic in which race, colour, and religion are the grounds of very arbitrary distinctions. The President is still an autocrat in many ways, and retains much of the habit of command necessary in a military leader. Lately, for example, he autocratically appointed a member of the Executive Council without consulting the Raad, though this appointment is laid down in the Grondwet, or Constitution, as the prerogative of the Raad. But the President's influence over the Raad and over the people, always great when danger threatens the State and when the people rally to him as to a military leader, tends to diminish in peaceful times. During the recent disturbances President Kruger's influence was paramount, and in any measures to preserve the independence of the country he had practically *carte blanche* to do what he liked. Yet even this year in domestic matters he has not been able to carry out his wishes. He himself was opposed to the Bill for the total prohibition of liquor to natives, notwithstanding which the measure was passed by the Raad. He has, too, in practice to conform very largely to the will of the people, and his influence is really due to the knowledge of their character and the closeness of his contact with them which enable him justly to appreciate what that will is. Any Boer may come up and have his talk with the President; and the absence of social distinctions and the smallness of the population—the Boer population of the Transvaal, as I have said, only being equal to that of a small county like Westmoreland—render personal contact between President and people all the more possible.

In spite, then, of the tendency to despotism which constant war and the accompanying subordination of the whole people might have produced, and which actually is shown in the attitude of the Boers towards aliens and natives, the opposite inherent tendency of the Boers to individual freedom has resulted in the formation of a representative agency, called the

Volksraad, for the expression of the will of the people; and this popular assembly is gaining an increasing control over the chief of the State. Mr. Kruger, on account of the exceptional history of the State, has become a sort of permanent President, having been in power now for fifteen years. He has, therefore, a special influence over the Raad which no future President is likely to possess. But there is no tendency to make the Presidentship hereditary; and, while a certain amount of stability is thus sacrificed, for there may be risks of contests for the Presidency after the manner of South American Republics, yet efficiency is obtained, for on the whole the best man is elected to be head of the State, and the people preserve their voice in the matter.

For the election of members of the Raad every male citizen of the State over sixteen years of age is entitled to vote, and in practice the voice of the people is very strongly felt. Members are paid, and are regarded by their constituents very much as delegates who must vote on any particular measure strictly according to the wishes of their constituencies. Government must publish any Bills they wish to introduce three months before the commencement of the Session; so that the people may have a chance of discussing them. And both before and after the Session members have to meet their constituents to discuss such Bills with them, to ascertain their wishes before the Session commences, and render an account of their stewardship after it has closed. The people can also make themselves heard by means of petitions addressed to the Volksraad. Several hundreds of such petitions, some signed by only a dozen or so of men, some signed by large numbers, and varying in importance from a request to have an obnoxious minor official removed from a particular locality to a demand that no newcomer under any pretext or pretence whatever should be allowed to have a share in the control of the country with the chosen people of God, have to be considered and reported on, and, if necessary, acted on by the Raad.

The people then, through the Raad, have a considerable voice in the conduct of affairs; and the Raad, by a vote of censure, can remove a President; as they did Pretorius in 1871. But the exact functions of the Raad, notwithstanding the clearness with which they are laid down in the Grondwet, are still very vaguely understood. In the old days—forty years ago, for that is old in South Africa—the Raad was also the highest executive authority, and there is still an inclination in the Raad to perform administrative duties in addition to their proper legislative work. The Executive, on the other hand, with an autocratically inclined President at their head, who frequently comes down to the Raad and storms at the members as if they were military subordinates, resent the legitimate control of the Raad.

Again, in regard to the distinction between judicial functions on the one hand and legislative or executive functions on the other, the line is still very roughly drawn in this Republic. The Raad is frequently interfering with the Grondwet. By, perhaps, only the casting vote of the Chairman the Raad will pass a resolution which they consider should have all the force of law. Many of these resolutions are contrary to the articles of the Constitution; and the Courts of Justice have then to decide whether, in cases which are brought before them, they are to abide by the hasty resolutions of the Raad or to follow the articles of the Constitution. If they choose the latter they are brought into direct opposition with the popular Assembly, and a contest between the two may at any time arise over a case now before the Courts. The action of the Court, too, is sometimes, though not frequently, interfered with by the Executive, who have on one or two occasions practically annulled the sentence of the Court by payment of the fine inflicted or by other means. Boer legislators and rulers find difficulty in recognising the absolute independence of Courts of law, and in ridding themselves of the idea that the Courts ought to be subject to them.

These, then, are the main principles upon which the State is governed. The practical administration, both in the judicial and executive branches, is in the hands of salaried foreigners or non-burghers. Not one of the Judges, and very few even of the holders of minor judicial posts, are Transvaal Boers. And though in the Executive Council only one member—the State Secretary—is a foreigner, nearly the whole of the administrative staff is composed of Hollanders or Cape-Colonial born Dutch Africanders. There are so few Transvaal Boers of sufficient education to serve in a Government office that it has been found necessary to hire foreigners to carry on the detailed work of the public offices; and many of the departments are under the Hollander State Secretary, to whom are also intrusted the foreign relations of the State, subject, it is commonly reported, to but slight control by the President and Executive Council, and to practically none by the Raad, except in that treaties have to be ratified by this latter body.

As regards the general efficiency of the Administration, opinions must differ according to the point of view. The Boers certainly have no reason to complain of it in so far as regards its effects on themselves; for it has proved itself capable of carrying them through a serious crisis, and as Government interferes but little with their liberties in peace times and taxes them very lightly, they are satisfied. But if the Government is strong because at its head are men of common sense, with much experience in troublous times, it is also (as I will show when I come to consider the position of the alien portion of the population) very slow in its movements and irresponsive to the calls of a young and rising country.

There are nowhere the signs of businesslike administration which Europeans expect, and the whole is subject to one very serious defect—the want of proper financial control, due to the fact that the finances are not controlled by the people who furnish the money. Quite nine-tenths of the revenue is derived from the industry of aliens. The Boers, therefore, feel no direct responsibility, and the necessity for economy is never brought home to them. They can spend large sums of money in secret service; they can purchase guns, rifles, and ammunition; they can hire trained foreigners to fill their public offices, to educate their children, and superintend the scientific branches of their army; they can build palatial government offices, courts of justice, national schools, forts, and barracks, even in a year when they have had to disburse £300,000 in precautionary measures against rinderpest; and can be as extravagant as they please, without any direct consequences in the form of additional taxes falling upon themselves. And apart from the debilitating effect such conduct must have on the national character, it is evident that the members of the Raad have no proper incentive to adequate control of the finances of the country, and the results of any particular policy can never be clearly appreciated by the mass of the people. This is a radical defect, which is bound to eat into the vitals of the people, and be a greater danger to their independence than any open attack which has yet been made upon them.

CHAPTER V

THE UITLANDERS

So far the Boer portion only of the white population of the Transvaal has been considered, but the Boers are only a minority of the white inhabitants, and, in addition to the 70,000 or 80,000 Boers, there are 130,000 or 140,000 white men of other nationalities resident in the country, though allowed no share in its government. With the discoveries of gold thousands of immigrants began streaming into the country, till they outnumbered the original Boer inhabitants; and it is these Uitlanders—the population, numerically stronger than the European population of India, yet treated as aliens by the Boers, who arrived in the country a few years previously—whose characteristics, work, and organisation I would now describe.

The idea of a Uitlander which possessed the mind of the British public, at any rate up to last year, and which is perhaps not yet entirely removed, was that of a swashbuckler in his shirt sleeves, with heavy riding boots, a large-brimmed hat turned up at one side like a lady's, and wearing a revolver at his belt. This is the Uitlander of the stage and of cartoons in *Punch.* Types of the different classes of the *real* Uitlander may be seen any day on the London Stock Exchange, in City banking and commercial offices, in Midland mining centres, around drinking bars, and in the audiences of London music-halls. The Uitlanders of the Transvaal are not the rough diggers of old Californian days familiar to readers of Bret Harte; nor are they bushmen of the Australian type; they are the ordinary—or perhaps the least successful—speculators, business men, clerks, and miners of any European country suddenly removed from Europe to make money more rapidly in South Africa.

If the chief object of the Boers in coming to the Transvaal was to obtain independence, the principal object that the Uitlanders have come for is this of making money. The Boers wanted independence first and money afterwards; the Uitlanders money first and independence if they could get it as well. Both have gained their main object—the Boers their independence and the Uitlanders their money—and by the same means, by strong persistent effort and marvellous perseverance. Gold in the Transvaal has not been found lying about waiting to be picked up. A small proportion was found in the form of nuggets, but even that was only discovered after long search and many hardships; and the vastly larger proportion is scattered in the finest grains among the rocks hundreds of feet below the surface of the ground. The minute grains of gold in the ordinary "reefs" are scarcely visible to the eye, and would never be noticed by a casual observer. Yet it is these hardly-perceptible grains which form the wealth of the Rand. Millions of tons of rock are brought up every year from the bowels of the earth and then crushed and sifted and chemically treated on the surface, till out of every ton of rock some two-and-a-half sovereigns or so are obtained; and the visitor who, looking at the open, grassy downs on which these gold mines are sunk, and passing from these innocent-looking steppes, on which the Boers could discover nothing else than fodder for their cattle, descends the shaft of a mine for a thousand or more feet till he is shown a faint streak of a particular rock in which he pretends to believe he can see gold; and who then watches tons of this gold-bearing rock, and the vastly larger quantity of barren rock which has also to be excavated to get at the good rock, being hauled to the surface, and then, ascending, looks at the powerful machinery and great stamps employed in crushing the rock to powder, the arrangement for roughly sifting the few golden grains from the mass of useless powder, and the refined chemical processes for extracting just another grain or two from the tons of seemingly valueless powder thrown aside by the sifter—the visitor who marks all this marvels at the energy and enterprise and scientific skill required to produce the magnificent results which the industry furnishes. And he wonders still more when he reflects that this industry was started before ever the railway had reached the Transvaal; when all the heavy machinery, the timber, the corrugated iron with which the works and men's houses are constructed, and nearly every requirement of work and of life had to be brought for over 300 miles upon ox-waggons, the country itself supplying scarcely a thing, and even to this day wheat being brought from Australia.

Yet now, where a dozen years ago there was nothing but bare veldt, hundreds of mines are at work, turning out more than eight millions sterling of gold and over a million tons of coal annually. On these mines one-and-a-half million pounds a year are spent in wages to Europeans and a similar amount to natives; half a million is expended in coal; half a million in explosives, &c.; and half a million in stores. Railways have been constructed from the coast in three different directions. A town with a population of 51,000 whites and 51,000 blacks has sprung up to furnish residences for and supply the needs of the mining community. And if the streets of this town are as bad as they well could be; if even now there are nearly a thousand houseless men who have to seek shelter where they can at night; and if the greater number of the houses are mere tin shanties, there are also public buildings, such as the Hospital, the Stock Exchange, the Chamber of Mines, the Rand Club, and there are houses of the larger companies and private residences fully on a par with the buildings of a European town. And besides the great stores of mining material and ironmongery there are clothing and millinery shops not much smaller than those of Regent Street, large grocery establishments, and even furniture shops from Bond Street and dress-making and sweet shops from Paris. Ladies of the richer class drive out in the best English carriages with their liveried English coachmen, and their drawing rooms are as comfortably and luxuriously furnished as the residences of any English town.

If, then, the Uitlanders are characterised by a gambling spirit which makes them nervous and excitable in comparison with their more stolid neighbours, and which shows itself not only in the share speculation of the richer, but among all classes and in nearly every branch of life; and if from having had to fight their way through the mass of unprincipled men who flock to a gold field, and from leading a life free from the restraints of social opinion usually exercised in more settled countries, few among them can be put down as either honest or truthful; their wonderful enterprise and initiative must be admitted, and not many could be found who have not had to work hard, risk much, and often undergo privation to gain their money. Industry is as characteristic of the Uitlander as indol-ence is of the Boer. Great houses like those of Wernher, Beit, Barnato, or J. B. Robinson have depended upon keen hard work and clear-sighted, far-seeing speculation for their success. And leading men like Mr. Samuel Marks or Mr. George Farrar have not gained their present wealth and influence by simple luck, but by sheer energy and pluck. They have had failure to encounter as well as success, but they have never sat still under failure. And a characteristic of the Uitlanders, which has as much significance as their excitability and impatience at not gaining political ends as rapidly as they gain their money, is their determined persistence. If they do not achieve their object one way they try another. But, one way or other, in the long run they gain what they are aiming at.

The Uitlanders are held together by few of the influences that serve to unite the Boers. They are not of one nationality, but about half are British, and there are large numbers of Germans, Americans, and Hollanders, and besides these Frenchmen, Italians, and Poles in lesser proportion. The Jewish element is, too, very prominent, the leading men especially being as much Jewish as British, German, or French, and giving a clearly Jewish tendency to both financial and political transactions. So the Uitlander population is thoroughly cosmopolitan, and, as I shall have occasion to emphasise later on, as thoroughly republican also, with no desire to remain under the government of their respective countries—the English under Downing-street, or the Germans under their Emperor. They have no religion nor strong family ties or family feeling to unite them, as we have seen these influences tend to unite the Boers; for practically the only religion of the Uitlander is the religion of work, and the greater proportion are unmarried or have left their wives behind. Nor have the Uitlanders had experience of that military co-operation which has been the main cause of union among the Boers.

But though they feel none of these influences which keep the Boers together, they have brought with them from Europe the business principles of modern countries, and they know the value of voluntary co-operation in the midst of competition. They possess, therefore, the faculty of which the Boers know nothing—of voluntary combination; and as a result from this they have individuality and initiative. Among the Boers there is not a single free combination for either commercial, philanthropic, religious, social, or scientific purposes. The Boers only know combination forced on them by external pressure. With the Uitlanders co-operation is as noticeable as their jealousies and keenness of rivalry; and the tendency is to continually greater combinations, as the great Gold Fields Company and the Barnato Amalgamation show. There are the Chambers of Mines and of Commerce, the Mercantile Association, the Association of Mine Managers, Freemasonry Lodges, Geological and Chemical Societies, and so on. And though at the beginning of last year there was a split in the Chamber of Mines, due probably to the racial feeling between Germans and English then prevalent, this has not prevented a general and remarkably successful combination among the mining companies to reduce the rate of native wages. Everywhere there are evidences of capacity for organisation. The rapid success of the mining operations sufficiently shows this; and the contrast in the capacity for organisation between the Boer Government and the Uitlanders was particularly striking on the occasion of the great dynamite explosion. The explosion occurred on trucks of the Dutch Railway Company, and the victims were nearly all Dutch. But though the Dutch Government officials were most anxious and willing to afford relief, while they were slowly revolving in their minds what to do, the Uitlander population had called a meeting, and, three hours after the accident, had subscribed £40,000 and organised a temporary hospital, medical staff, and relief parties.

And here parenthetically I may notice the generosity and hospitality of the Uitlanders. Men who make money quickly are proverbially free in parting with it, and the Uitlanders are especially liberal in that respect. I personally have much to thank them for in the great hospitality shown me—a hospitality which I gratefully acknowledge, but which will, I hope, not influence me in truthfully depicting the situation in this country. Their business is carried on less by letter than by word of mouth. They therefore know each other well, and are always genial in their social intercourse.

In so far, then, as the Uitlanders, not being formed into a separate State, possess organisation, that organisation has many elements of efficiency. The leaders are usually the best men among them, or, if some are not, their places are easily filled by those who are. There has not been sufficient time for the formation of strong vested interests, and there are no antiquated institutions standing in the way of useful development. As a body, Uitlanders lack the steadying effect which old-established institutions and tradition give, but they have the advantage of being able readily to adapt themselves to new requirements. Even the same companies and same individuals take up gold mining, coal mining, fruit growing, or tree planting with equal readiness. And this adaptability to the needs of the occasion is as likely to show itself in political life as it has already in industrial.

The Uitlanders have not either that military or political experience which the Boers have gained during the last half century of strenuous national life. They have been too much engrossed in business, and too little in touch with public life apart from business, to furnish good public men. But just as hard as the Boers have fought for the independence of the Transvaal the Uitlanders are now working for its material development. Work is combining the Uitlanders as war has combined the Boers. And the future prosperity of the country depends upon whether those who have worked and those who have fought for it may be welded together in one united community.

CHAPTER VI

THE RELATIONS BETWEEN BOERS AND UITLANDERS

THE characteristics of the country and of the two sections of the white population have been described, and it now remains to give some account of the relations which exist between these two sections. Most people are aware that the enterprising Uitlander population, who have made the bare prairies of the Transvaal bring forth millions of gold and lifted the original Boer population from a state of abject poverty to one of easy affluence, are treated by these same Boers strictly as aliens; but few, probably, have realised that these skilled and educated Europeans, accustomed to the most advanced forms of political freedom, are treated with considerably less liberality than are the natives of India by the British Government. Yet such is the case, and a comparison between the degree of liberty enjoyed by the Uitlanders in the Transvaal and the degree of liberty accorded to the natives of India will help to illustrate the precise position of the former. In India on the Legislative Councils of the Viceroy and of the Governors of provinces there is always a proportion of native members; and native members of Council have lately been accorded the right of questioning the financial expenditure of the Government. There are native Judges even in the High Courts; there are native members of the Administration; and there are more than 700 municipalities in Indian towns. In the Transvaal municipal rights have not yet been granted to a single town; 130,000 or so of Uitlanders will this year contribute about five millions to the revenue of the country, yet, far from being accorded any control over the expenditure of this large sum of money, they have not even an official means of expressing an opinion upon it—nay, more, by the new Press Law they may be prevented from expressing disapproval even in newspapers, and these very lines may be forbidden re-entrance to this country. And the mining industry is not represented in the Government even by a Dutch official; for though there is a Dutch Minister of Mines he is not given a seat on the Executive Council—the Commandant-General and the Superintendent of Natives receiving a seat before him. Even Kaffirs in Cape Colony and negroes in America have greater freedom than the Uitlanders in the Transvaal; and the single way in which the Uitlanders may be represented is in the second Volksraad. After expressly renouncing his former country, after becoming liable to military service, the Uitlander may obtain the single privilege of membership in a body which has no control over the finances of the country, and whose resolutions upon other points are liable to veto by the first Volksraad.

The attitude of the Boer rulers to the alien population is therefore thoroughly consonant with the military tendencies of their form of government. It is absolutely despotic. The Boer is to be the ruler, the Uitlander the worker, and each is to be separate from the other. This is not the attitude which the Boers have always taken up towards the newcomers, for time was when any one who had lived for a year in the country might enjoy all the privileges of the first Boer arrivals. Up to 1885 residents of five years' standing were granted similar privileges. But since the rush of immigrants to the gold fields commenced the laws have gradually been increased in stringency, till now an almost impassable barrier has been set up between the new comer and the old. The Boers have feared that if every one who came to the country received full political privileges as easily as had formerly been possible, they would very soon be swamped out by the incoming tide; and they believe even now (for the President insisted on the point to me) that the Uitlanders only come here for a short time to make money as rapidly as they can and leave the country; and the Boers argue that, if they were allowed any share in its government, they would seek to introduce measures, not for the real future good of the country, but to enable them to make money still more rapidly than they make it at present and return all the sooner to Europe. This, too, is the view, not only of the extreme Conservatives, but also of the most progressive members of the Raad. Again, the President, on both my visits, laid stress on the fact that when a few years ago Uitlanders were asked to join in a campaign against the native chief Maloboch they nearly all refused. Mr. Kruger does not accept as an explanation of this refusal that at the time they were asked to fight for the country they had no assurance that they would be allowed the privileges of citizenship in it. So much of his life having been spent in fighting for this country he seems to consider that fighting for it is the only method of showing loyalty, and that those who have worked industrially for its welfare have no claim upon it. He says, too, that it is impossible to trust the miscellaneous assortment of humanity which flocks to the gold fields, and points to the many evidences of hostility to the Boer Government which the mining population have shown, the result of which has been to imbue the Boer mind with profound suspicion of the newcomers.

The Boers, then, sit over in Pretoria and legislate, and the Uitlanders mass together round Johannesburg and work, but the two remain completely separate; and, while the attitude of the Boers towards the newcomers is one of deep suspicion, the attitude of the Uitlanders is still one of sullen discontent towards their unprogressive rulers. There are still in the Transvaal many British subjects who fought against the Boers in 1880, and who preserve much of the bitterness of feeling which war engenders; and there are numbers in the country who would gladly seize any opportunity of wiping out certain memories which gall upon them. At times when the market is low, and when there are large numbers out of employment, as there will be with the present rush of immigration if the market remains low and so causes business to slacken, serious trouble might very easily arise from this section of the community. But besides this inflammable portion of the Uitlander population there are numbers of Germans, French, and Americans who have no such reasons for race animosity, and who, as they are at present obtaining favours from the Boers because these latter are anxious to alienate them from the British section, have no wish to disturb the present *régime*. And even among the British portion there are many who would prefer things as they are, rather than risk the chance of further troubles such as occurred a short time ago.

There are, then, tendencies which, fortunately, keep in check the antagonism between the races which undoubtedly exists; and another influence of the same description comes from the fact that, while the Boer Government has shown during recent years an inclination towards increased political separation between themselves and the Uitlanders, the tendency has not been towards increased obstruction to the mining industry on its economic side. There is no actual encouragement of the mining industry, and the most that the Boer Government does is to sanction a few of the many proposals which the Uitlanders make to them for the development of the industry; they have, for instance, condescended to allow the mining companies to make a metalled road along the Rand at their own expense. Still the Gold Law is liberal, and has been improved from year to year, Government have helped rather than obstructed the mines in the procuring and regulation of native labour; and, while nervous lest the mining industry should outgrow their capacity to control it, they have no deliberate policy of strangling it, as they have not yet entirely forgotten what the revenue of the country was before the opening of the mines, and have no wish to see it again drop from £5,000,000 to £75,000.

At one time there were several indications of what might be considered an exactly opposite intention on the part of Government, and more genuine discontent was caused among the Uitlanders than I think at any previous time. The pegging-out by Government officials of claims on property which mining companies have possessed for years;

and the declaration of intention to enforce certain provisions of the Sunday Law which have hitherto been held in abeyance, coming immediately after oppressive political measures like the Press Law and the Expulsion of Aliens Bill, have caused many to think that a deliberate set is being made to ruin or curtail the industry. Yet in spite of these harassing measures, which have done much to shake confidence in the Government, I think that the chief charges which the mining industry, as an industry, might justly bring against the Government are of indifference and ignorance, rather than of deliberate and intentional obstruction.

Reviewing the situation, we have then a strong but slow-moving and unprogressive section of the population controlling another section double them in numbers, and energetic, enterprising, and impatient. The indolent section believes it only wishes to be let alone, but does not object to sucking what sweets the presence of the working section affords; and this working section believes it wants political power, but in reality only wants to be allowed to work without hindrance. The Boers are suspicious of the Uitlanders aiming to get the government in their hands, and the rough farmers shudder at the idea of being controlled by stock-jobbers from Europe; while the money-seeking Uitlanders, realising the enormous possibilities of wealth which the country affords were the

Government but intelligent and progressive, chafe at the obstacles to development which the Boers place in their way or refuse to remove. The Boers consider that they have fought for the country and that it is theirs by right; and when it is remembered that only a few years ago the very men who sit in the Rand at Pretoria and legislate for the Uitlanders were out on commando with rifles in their hands fighting for their independence, it is easy to imagine how determined they would be to keep the government in their hands. The Uitlanders are at perfect liberty to come and make money and furnish the Boers with funds, but they must expect no share in the government of the country.

The resulting condition of affairs is not satisfactory, and might cause serious anxiety were the Boers hot-headed and irascible. But, after all, their chief defect is only unprogressiveness, and we have the experience of the Cape Colony, Natal, and the Free State that Boers and British can work harmoniously together. I hope, therefore, to be able to show that there are lines of possible development which do not necessarily involve the violent uprisings which I have now to describe, and which took place soon after my arrival in Johannesburg.

CHAPTER VII

THE CRISIS IN JOHANNESBURG

THE foregoing chapter will have given an idea of the general position of affairs in the Transvaal; and when I arrived in Johannesburg in the middle of December, 1895, the antagonism between the two races—British and Dutch—between enterprise and stolidity—was fast approaching a climax. Everywhere, in the train, in the hotel, in the club, the same story was told me. The pushing, energetic Uitlander was fretting under the restrictions placed upon his enterprise by the stolid Boer rulers of the country; and chafing under their hopeless immobility and inability to provide the proper administration for a great mining and business centre. The newspapers representing the forward section daily published articles silently attacking the Boer Government. And the vague apprehension that trouble was brewing quickly increased in vividness till men began to send their wives and children away from the town, and the crisis came nearer and nearer.

On December 26th, Charles Leonard, as Chairman of the Transvaal National Union, issued a Manifesto in which he stated that in view of the momentous issue to be faced, a review of the position prior to the holding of a general meeting on January 6th was necessary. The Manifesto pointed out that the objects of the Union were the maintenance of the independence of the Republic, the securing of equal rights, and the redress of grievances. It stated that the Uitlanders were the majority in the State; owned more than half the land and at least nine-tenths of the property; yet in all matters affecting their lives, their liberties, and their properties they had absolutely no voice.

The Manifesto concludes:—"We desire an independent Republic which shall be a true Republic, in which every man who takes the oath of allegiance to the State shall have equal rights, and in which our children shall be brought up side by side as united members of a strong commonwealth. We are animated by no race hatred. We desire to deprive no man, be his nationality what it may, of any right. We want:—

1. The establishment of the Republic as a true Republic.

2. A Grondwet or Constitution, which shall be framed by competent persons selected by representatives of the whole people, and framed on lines laid down by them—a Constitution which shall be safeguarded against hasty alterations.

3. An equitable franchise, law, and fair representation.

4. Equality of the Dutch and English languages.

5. Responsibility to the Legislature of the heads of the great departments.

6. The removal of religious disabilities.

7. The independence of the Court of Justice, with adequate and secured remuneration for the Judges.

8. Liberal and comprehensive education.

9. An efficient Civil Service, with adequate provision for pay and pensions.

10. Free trade in South African products.

What the situation in Johannesburg was at the time of the publication of the Manifesto will best be made clear by an extract from a letter I wrote to the *Times* (published January 25th, 1896), dated December 28th, and actually despatched from Johannesburg on the very day that Jameson crossed the border. This extract will, I think, show the views which Sir Hercules Robinson had expressed to me at Cape Town, that Johannesburg would not of itself resort to arms was a correct one. After first giving a summary of the Manifesto and its claim, and quoting Mr. Leonard's concluding appeal that as to how these claims were to be obtained he expected an answer in plain terms to be given at the great mass meeting to be held on January 6th, I wrote :—

"It is just this question of 'How?' that is producing so much difference of opinion in Johannesburg at the present time. That the Manifesto contains a fair summary of grievances every one is agreed. The position here is indeed intolerable to men accustomed, as the greater part of the Uitlander community have been, to live under highly organised Governments, free institutions, and amid civilisation generally of the most advanced type. From the first moment of entering the country a suppressed feeling of irritation is felt at the dilatoriness and slovenliness on the railway, the signs of municipal neglect in the town, the vexatious state of affairs at the post office and telegraph office. And the settler in the country finds this feeling of irritation increase as he struggles on against the gross mismanagement and deadly hostility to his interests which prevail; as he finds even necessaries of life taxed till prices have become almost prohibitive; as he sees restrictions imposed on labour which cramp his mining enterprises, and the prices of necessities for his work doubled through monopolies. There is not a Uitlander in the place who does not feel some irritation at the existing condition of things, some annoyance at the evident mismanagement, some longing to have matters put more straight. On this point all are agreed, all feel that there are legitimate causes of complaint, and that the Union Manifesto is a true statement of the grievances.

It is only upon the question as to how the claims for the redress of these grievances are to be put forward that opinions differ so widely at present.

"It is everywhere stated that large quantities of arms have been imported into Johannesburg, that Maxim guns have been brought in amongst machinery, and that one party intend to have recourse to force to effect their ends. This active policy evidently, however, does not meet with the approval of the majority of the inhabitants of Johannesburg. They have too much at stake. They have their wives and children to look after. They have immense properties here. The closing down of the mines, the stagnation of trade, a rich town at the mercy of the mob and of the thousands of natives who would be let loose, and who, breaking into the liquor shops, might cause unspeakable trouble—all these are evils which the majority of the Uitlanders say they will not face. They say they would rather bear the ills they have than fly to others that they know not of. Some even go further and say that if any section of the community does raise a revolt they will themselves try to stop it by the use of arms. The old saying that Englishmen are never so peacefully employed as when they are engaged in making money is fully borne out here at the present time. The inhabitants of Johannesburg are not a seditious, rebellious, quarrelsome set of men. They are money-makers. Rebellion and money-making do not go together. So the feeling now is certainly against rebellion ; and unless the Boer is either more clever or more intensely stupid than he is given credit for, he will never goad the Uitlander to take up arms against him.

"But it must not be imagined from this that the Uitlander will not press his claims. The same argument which applies against his having recourse to force applies equally in favour of his persisting by every other means to gain his objects. Money is not to be made so plentifully, business cannot be carried on so surely, under a Government like the present. Men whose whole training consists in seeing that money spent brings in its proper return cannot remain impassive under a system by which money taken from them is spent, without any sort of control, in the most reckless and unprofitable way. So they must, and they will, go on agitating for reform. They none of them want to see the British flag hoisted here. They none of them want to see the present Republic done away with. There is not a sign among the Uitlanders of the Transvaal of any agitation in that direction. There is no wish to turn out the Boers, and, with all that is said against Boer government, for the Boers as a people much respect and sympathy are felt. In spite of their faults as rulers they are looked upon as a brave and hardy people, and their rights as the first pioneers in this country are recognised. There is no wish, then, on the part of the Uitlanders to break down the Republic and make a British colony of the Transvaal. But they want to have a true Republic governed by the people who live in it; to make the Boers realise that, though they were the first arrivals, they must not hold the country exclusively to themselves against the thousands, and it will soon be hundreds of thousands, who are following after; to have the Transvaal for Boer and Uitlander alike, till the term 'Uitlander'—outsider—is done away with, and the present oligarchy gives place to a Republic in the true sense of the term.

"If there were any assurance or hope that patience would effect their ends, the Uitlanders would resort to it. But they have no such hope. They know well that they have to deal with no pliable 'give-and-take' description of people, but with a hard, unyielding race blessed, like many of the British race also, with the virtue of 'pig-headedness,' and led by an autocratic President, in whom the virtues and the faults of the race are combined in a superlative degree. Against this race the Uitlanders have no real animosity. They know the Boers have not all the beautiful traits of character with which those who only know them from a distance credit them. They know that with all their religiousness they are notoriously untruthful, that with their love of independence there is mixed an indolent shrinking from the competition of life among civilised nations, and that the spirit of enterprise and progress in civil life has in consequence dried up in them. Still they see in the Boers qualities which everywhere command admiration. They see a people who, rather than submit to the exactions imposed upon them nearly three centuries ago, were willing to leave their homes and friends in Europe to spend their lives in lands immeasurably more distant and infinitely less known than South Africa is at the present day—a people who again left their new homes to wander far into the interior, and amongst hostile tribes, to seek a country where they might be free, and who in this land have maintained their freedom against both the savages and a powerful civilised nation. The Uitlanders recognise that these Boers must be a brave and hardy people ; and though there is at present a feeling of exasperation which soon may grow into animosity, there is as yet no such animosity among the Uitlanders.

"But the Uitlanders feel that to gain their rights they must be as obstinate as the Boers themselves, that they must go on urging and pressing their claims ; and before the energy and perseverance which exist in the characters of the British, the Americans, the Germans, and the French who make up the 130,000 Uitlanders the 40,000 Boers must in the end give way."

Meanwhile the excitement and uneasiness in the

town increased. Notices that arms were being imported into the town appeared daily in the papers, and allusions even appeared to the presence of Jameson and his men on the frontier. They were there for something, and the arms were being imported with some hidden object. The sense of the town was against fighting; but fighting might evidently come, and so many thought it desirable to clear out while they still might. The trains down country were crammed many hours before the time of starting. Even goods trucks were filled with people. And something like a panic was setting in when on Monday, December 30th, the evening newspaper, the *Star*, announced that Dr. Jameson had crossed the border and was marching into the Transvaal.

I well remember the looks of utter dumbfoundedness with which the news was received. It simply took men's breath away: the audacity of the move, and the awful consequences which it might involve. And upon none did it produce a greater sense of consternation than on the leaders of the political agitation, who knew that Jameson was on the border ready, if need be, to help them, but who for weeks past had been making every possible effort to prevent his marching before they themselves were ready. They had indeed, more than a month previous to this, written him and delivered into his hands when he was himself at Johannesburg in the middle of November, a provisional letter to be acted on in case of a necessity. This letter was the famous "women and children" letter. It called upon him to come to the aid of Johannesburg *should disturbance arise.* But the disturbance had not so far arisen. Moreover, Johannesburg was not yet ready, even if it were willing, to take up arms and strike a blow for liberty because those arms had not yet arrived. A few hundreds of stands of arms had indeed reached the town, but the bulk was still delayed on account of the block in the railway, and the three Maxims did not arrive till two days after Dr. Jameson had actually started.

The position of the Johannesburg leaders at this time was one of extraordinary perplexity. They themselves no doubt felt acutely the obstructiveness of the Boers. They were responsible for the profitable working of large enterprises. They saw that those enterprises were not paying anything like the dividends which they might pay under a proper Government; and as the Government had shown no signs during the last year of making any concessions, the agitators for reform had eagerly caught up the idea of resorting to arms in order to put pressure on Government, and when outside assistance was proffered they were not slow to accept it.

But the great mass of the people were not at that time discontented, though most have since become so. The ordinary miner, the business employé and the clerks were all getting very high wages, which might very possibly be reduced if large numbers of men were attracted to the country by good government. There were certainly then no open signs of seething sedition among what would have to form the rank and file if revolution there was to be. And it was difficult for the leaders to approach the men to ascertain their views about taking up arms without divulging too much of their plans. Certain it is that on the Monday morning on which Jameson was crossing into the Transvaal, in the teeth of the remonstrances of the Johannesburg leaders, and without having given them any warning of his intentions, the leaders on comparing notes found they had only three or four hundred men on whom they could depend, and they knew all the time that the Boer Government was aware of their intentions.

But while there were immense risks in resorting to arms there were evident signs of the Transvaal Government yielding to a certain extent and of the Uitlanders being able to obtain, without actual fighting, a great part of what *they* wanted. There was gradually growing among a section of the Boers a feeling that President Kruger was persisting too steadfastly in his rigid policy of exclusiveness. Dutchmen of the Orange Free State, the Cape Colony and Natal even, accounted Uitlanders the same as any new arrival from England or America. And these Dutchmen were beginning to make their influence felt upon their *confrères* in the Transvaal till many of these latter were saying that Government ought to relax a little. Moreover the exaggerated accounts of the number of rifles, Maxims and guns which were being imported into Johannesburg were having their effect upon Government, who began to see that they had been too unyielding, and might be on the verge of more serious trouble than they were able to cope with. Nor could Government have then counted on the support of the whole Boer population in suppressing any spontaneous rising in Johannesburg, for many were openly saying that if the President was obstinate enough to set the fire alight he might himself put it out. Indeed, when the orders were sent to the district to mobilise, one district, not having heard that it was in order to resist an outside invasion, but thinking it was merely to suppress an outbreak in Johannesburg, flatly refused to obey the summons. It was only when they were informed that the object was to defend their country from a foreign invasion that they obeyed.

On the eve, then, of the Jameson raid, the Government, recognising the symptoms of coming trouble, showed signs of bending before the storm. President Kruger issued a proclamation removing duties on food stuffs, and he promised to submit to the Volksraad proposals to grant equal subsidies to the English and Dutch schools and full franchise to all who declared for the Government in the crisis. This was not much. It was mostly promises, and President Kruger's promises are not much relied on by the people of Johannesburg. But the Johannesburg leaders had little confidence that they would be able to effect anything better by a premature revolution. The only chance of success that there had ever been lay in a surprise and a sudden night attack upon the undefended arsenal at Pretoria and the drawing of the teeth of the Boers by the capture of the artillery in the arsenal.

Now that the Government were on the alert this was out of the question, and the Boers being better armed and organised than the Johannesburgers the latter would have no chance of success in a conflict, and their best hope lay in making the utmost of the fear which the known presence of arms in Johannesburg must produce. The Government would be able to gather from the fact that arms had been collected, that the Uitlanders meant business, and that there was cause to be careful about offending them further.

When, then, the Johannesburg leaders received about midday on Monday an obscure private telegram from Mafeking, announcing that the "veterinary doctor" had started and might be backed for "seven hundred" pounds, they were utterly dismayed. Now "the fat was in the fire," and they were not surprised when they shortly after intercepted an official telegram from Pretoria addressed to one of the Boer commandants, and ordering him to ride through Johannesburg and shoot right and left indiscriminately, to crush down the anticipated revolution before it had time to break out.

On the Tuesday my report was, "The news of the advance of an armed party from Bechuanaland is not very favourably received. There is no general wish in the community to resort to arms except in defence, and equally little wish to destroy the independence of the Republic."

Even the *Johannesburg Star*, the inspired organ of extreme agitationists, and the editor of which was a member of the Reform Committee, "joined with the morning journals in deploring the action of the Bechuanaland force in entering the Transvaal, and the letter of appeal to Dr. Jameson and the well-nigh hopeless construction which would be placed upon it." The *Star* "hoped that a tumult would be avoided and a national compromise adjusted."

What happened subsequently may be best told by quoting a long telegram[1] I sent from Pretoria on January 4th, recapitulating the daily telegrams I had been sending, and which I had reason to believe were being delayed. This telegram I do not hesitate to reproduce *in extenso*, as, written on the spot, it accurately records the state of feeling at the time.

[1] *Times*, January 10th, 1896.

CHAPTER VIII

THE REVOLT AND RAID

"On the morning of December 30th news was received in an obscure private telegram that Dr. Jameson's force had crossed the border into Transvaal territory.

"This was at first considered such an utterly impossible proceeding that no notice was taken of it; but when in the afternoon a local evening paper, the *Star*, issued a special edition with the news telegraphed from Pretoria, there was no longer any doubt about it. For that evening men simply stood aghast at the boldness of the move. Next morning shops and banks were open as usual, and at first it seemed as if there would be no more stir in Johannesburg than in any other town in South Africa over this startling news; but towards midday men were seen collecting round the office of the Reform Committee, and it became known that arms were to be served out to men who would enrol under the order of the Committee. At the same time the flag of the Transvaal Republic was

DOORNFONTEIN AND JOHANNESBURG.

[*To face page* 75.

hoisted over the building as a sign that arms were to be taken up, not with the object of doing away with the present Republic and turning it into a British colony, but with the fixed intention of keeping it as a Republic.

"This is the keynote of the present agitation, which is for internal reform, and not for the overthrow of the Republic.

"The town now began to be agitated. There were no signs of real excitement, for, though crowds collected, there was no noise, no hurried movements of men; but every one felt we were on the brink of some great action, the result of which it was impossible to foretell. The nerves of the town became more and more highly strung as armed men were formed up into parties and marched through the streets away to the heights on the north. It seemed as if the slightest spark would set the whole town alight, and that a bloody conflict would take place between the Uitlanders and the Dutch still in the town. A shot was heard, and close by where the sound came from three or four policemen were seen. A crowd rapidly collected, and it was thought that some tragic affair had taken place, but all that had happened was that a horse had tumbled down and been shot. Another shot was heard, but this time it was only a recruit letting off his rifle by mistake. On each occasion, however, there was a quiver of excitement, as it was feared that it might be the first shot in the conflict.

"Yet nothing was more remarkable than the quiet and orderly manner in which the whole movement, by which the control of the town passed, in a few hours, from the hands of the Government into the hands of the Reform Committee, was carried out. Probably men of no other two nationalities in the world could have carried out such a movement so quietly. Englishmen quietly armed themselves and marched stolidly off to their appointed places; Dutchmen noiselessly withdrew their police and concentrated at the goal; and from that day to this there has not been even a single brawl in the town. It was an astonishing sight to look from the windows and see the orderly crowds of men on that eventful night, when each one expected that before morning there must be a deadly struggle.

"Throughout the town, during the afternoon, people not only closed their shop doors, but boarded up their windows, and by the evening numbers of men came marching in from outlying mines, and were cheered as they passed through the streets. All through the afternoon mounted corps were being organised, men being served out with horses, brand new saddlery, and rifles, and then riding away to patrol round the outskirts of the town. Yet there was not the slightest sign of over-excitement in the streets; and the first, and therefore most critical, night passed by without a shot being fired in anger.

"On the following day, Tuesday, the organising

and drilling of newly-enrolled men was steadily proceeded with, and by this time a marked change of feeling had come over the town.

"Up to now it may be said with certainty that the majority had not wished to fight; they recognised that they had much to lose by it, and, being almost unarmed, how could they expect to effect anything by fighting against an organised Government? But when they saw rifles, and even Maxims, being served out, and an efficient organisation being formed, and when they heard that a strong body of highly-equipped troops, under daring leaders, had come across the border to aid them, then those who had before held aloof joined the organisation; they felt that they had now a chance, and, moreover, that if fighting should take place, as was now almost inevitable, it would be almost impossible to stand neutral.

"Until one actually sees it, it is hard to realise how strong is the tendency among a mass of men to fall together in circumstances such as these. For weeks past, and especially after the issue of the Manifesto, letters had been written to the newspapers denouncing in the strongest terms the folly of attempting to take up arms against the Government. Some had gone so far as to say that if any should attempt to do so they would forcibly oppose them. Organisations even had been formed for this express purpose; yet when the move was made, when arms actually were taken up, every one, with hardly an exception, joined in. Americans, and even Germans, who had formerly been so opposed to it, declared themselves ready to support it. The reason for this was evidently that men realised that they must be either on one side or the other in the struggle, and that they were safer with a rifle in their hands than without one.

"Finding evidently, therefore, that the organisation of the Reform Committee was a strong one, and that the Government, by allowing the control of the town to pass out of their hands, were apparently weak, they naturally clustered round the former, and far more men than they had need for came to the offices of the Committee asking to be enrolled. In this way the movement grew till practically the whole town was absorbed in it.

"On the evening of Tuesday, the 31st, a deputation was sent by the Government from Pretoria asking that a similar deputation might be sent to Pretoria to meet General Joubert and talk matters over with him, to see whether arrangements might not be come to; and it was agreed on both sides that neither should meanwhile take any action against the other, that Johannesburg should retain its defensive attitude, and that Pretoria would not attack it or invest it. There was, however, no agreement that action should not be taken against Dr. Jameson.

"A deputation, consisting of Mr. Lione Phillips,

PRETORIA.

[*To face page* 79.

Mr. Abe Bailey, and Mr. Auret, accordingly went to Pretoria early in the morning of January 1.

"Shortly before they left a telegram was received by the Committee from Sir Jacobus de Wet, the British Agent in Pretoria, repeating the substance of a proclamation by the High Commissioner repudiating Dr. Jameson's action, and calling upon all British subjects in the Transvaal to render him no assistance.

"After considering this communication, the Committee telegraphed to their representatives in Pretoria, authorising them to inform the Government that if they would allow Dr. Jameson to come into Johannesburg without opposing him they would guarantee with their lives to send him back. This was communicated to the Government. Nothing, however, was effected by the deputation, as in the meantime it had been arranged that the High Commissioner should come to Pretoria to effect a settlement; but the Reform Committee despatched a member to meet Dr. Jameson to hand him the High Commissioner's proclamation and to induce him to stop.

"On the afternoon of this day a rumour began to spread that Dr. Jameson's force was fighting the Boers near Krugersdorp, a small mining township twenty miles west of Johannesburg. Little doubt was felt that he must be successful, if not in forcing his way through the Boers, at any rate in getting round them, for he had with him a highly-equipped, magnificently-armed, and well-mounted corps, and the Boers had been taken completely by surprise, and had had no opportunity of collecting their men together.

"Every one in Johannesburg expected, therefore, that on the following day Dr. Jameson and his force would march triumphantly into the town; and so vividly had his daring appealed to the people that they would have given him an unparalleled ovation, accepted him as their future leader, and followed him unquestioningly through anything.

"On Thursday morning, the 2nd, a vague rumour came in that matters had not gone altogether so satisfactorily with him as had been at first reported; still, he was known to have now passed Krugersdorp, and crowds flocked out of the town to meet him.

"Riding along the road to Krugersdorp to reach the spot where fighting was said to be taking place, I found the road blocked by the Boer outposts, who were now occupying each village, but riding round them and then following at a distance a strong Boer patrol who were evidently making towards their main body, my companion (Mr. Heygate) and myself, on cresting the ridge, suddenly saw beneath us, near the hamlet of Vlakfontein, two bodies of men whom we thought were on the point of attacking each other, but as we stood there one party turned round and slowly marched back toward Krugersdorp.

"By the regularity of its movements we knew it could only be Dr. Jameson's force, yet even then we never thought that it could have surrendered, and it was only when we rode up to the Boer leader that we heard what had actually occurred.

"We were allowed to ride up to the retiring column, but not to converse with the officers and men, who were riding along in their shirt sleeves unarmed between escorts of Boers.

"They looked terribly tired, but were as hard and determined looking a lot as could be brought together, and the bravery which they had displayed earned the unstinted admiration of the Boers. What must have gone far to causing them to surrender was the fact that they were utterly exhausted; it was now ninety hours since they had started on their daring ride, and as in that time they had covered more than 160 miles of ground, had been engaged in hard scouting work, and for the last twenty-four hours had fought almost constantly, they had had but few hours' sleep and no time to spare for cooking, and consequently had to fight their last battle completely knocked up.

"They found the Boers posted behind ridges of rock, with long open slopes in front of them. It was impossible to get at them. They tried to pass by to the right, but were stopped, so they gradually got drawn into the shallow hollow. They could not force their way out, and they had to surrender.

"When the news of this surrender reached Johannesburg it caused the utmost depression. Dr. Jameson was known personally to numbers in the town; his popularity is remarkable, and, above all, it was felt that when he had started on this adventure to relieve the town, and had got to within thirteen miles of it, some effort ought to have been made to help him. A Scotch party of nearly 1,000 men wanted to go out there and then to rescue him; they said they would rather die than suffer the disgrace of leaving him, and they desisted only when consideration showed them that an heroic effort of that sort was hardly likely to be successful, and would only, if unsuccessful, make matters worse for Dr. Jameson and his officers, and possibly also cause the Boers to bombard Johannesburg.

"But that night an angry mob gathered round the offices of the Reform Committee, and roundly abused them for not sending out help, whether they had sufficient or not. The Military Committee especially were censured; but the whole movement being a political movement, they were in the hands of the main Reform Committee, the members of which had very good reasons for not acting. In the first place, they had not asked Dr. Jameson to come in when he did, and he embarrassed them greatly by doing so; in the second place, they had no idea that he stood so urgently in need of assistance; and, lastly, they were under the terms of an armistice pending the arrival of the High Commissioner. Nor is it altogether certain that any help they could send would have been effectual.

"It is probable that on the morning of the last fight, when considerable reinforcements had arrived from Pretoria, the Boers could have placed just as many men against the Johannesburg contingent as they did against Dr. Jameson. The Johannesburgers were merely a rabble with arms in their hands, and could have afforded little real assistance. Still, so great was Dr. Jameson's popularity, and so deep-felt the admiration for his daring, that, in spite of this, if it had been at all realised what straits he was in, thousands would have been ready to go out and succour him at any cost.

"Many people have said that the Boers have degenerated, and that the young Boer is not of the same stamp as those who have gone before. This may be so, but there are still many thousands of the old class left; all those I saw at Vlakfontein were of the rugged old stock, strong, hard-looking men, who went about their business in a cool, deliberate, one might almost say cold-blooded, way, as if they were born and bred to it. There were hundreds of these same men riding about Pretoria in their wideawake hats, ordinary coats and trousers, like any civilian, but with their rifles hung over their shoulders, cartridge belt round them, and small bag of provisions, which showed them ready to go off to fight at any moment. The rapidity with which these men collect, and the skill which they show in the choice of their positions, in their marksmanship, and in all operations of guerilla warfare, is marvellous.

"All these men are in the highest degree incensed against Dr. Jameson. They admire his bravery, but to attack without a quarrel they think unpardonable.

"Still more incensed are the Boers against the men who asked Dr. Jameson to come in; for on the person of one of the captured officers was a letter, signed by five of the leading men in Johannesburg, asking him to come.

"The surrender of these men is demanded. The more hot-headed of the Boers demand also the unconditional surrender of Johannesburg, the giving up of the arms in the hands of the mob, the handing over of the leaders, and the tearing up of the London Convention.

"These are among the conditions which the Boers will probably ask for, and they are massing men and guns up to Johannesburg to enforce them.

"There has probably never been a more difficult situation in South Africa; but one thing is certain—that the origin of the trouble is due to the Republican Government. However incensed they may be at much that has happened, they must acknowledge that, if they had ruled the country during the fifteen years of their existence in a manner in which it is expected that a civilised country should be ruled, the wealthy capitalists, who have so much to lose by disturbances such as have occurred, would never have been driven to adopt the course which they have adopted. Agitation for reform has been carried on in the most open manner possible. It is six weeks now since Mr. Lionel Phillips, in his outspoken deliverance, gave the first note of warning to the Government that resort to force might be made if some justice were not shown. In the Leonard Manifesto the Government had another significant warning, but it was not till December 30th that Johannesburg actually took up arms; and though it is now nearly a week since this was done, not one single act of hostility has been committed by the men of Johannesburg. They took up arms to show they were in earnest, and because they had been taught to realise that by nothing short of this could they obtain their just rights, the equal rights shown to every citizen of a civilised country. But by their very first act of hoisting the flag of this Republic they showed that they meant no disloyalty to the State, and by the control and the moderation which they have displayed since arming and by the readiness with which they met the proposals of the Government to discuss matters in Pretoria, they have given evidence of a determination to proceed as temperately as possible. It may be said that the existence of the letter calling in Dr. Jameson does not agree with all this show of moderation; but it is certain that though Dr. Jameson had a general letter asking him to help them in case of disturbance, the Committee had no wish for him to come in when he did; and as evidence that this was the case it has only to be borne in mind that they did all they could to induce him to go back, and offered to guarantee with their lives that he should do so.

"President Kruger will, no doubt, have great difficulty in controlling the angry men who have now risen to arms all over the country; but he has throughout this crisis distinguished himself by his moderation; and if now, by a further display of moderation, and by conceding something to the Uitlanders, he can avert the crisis, he will have saved a war which may begin with disaster, but which could not end there."

CHAPTER IX

AFTER THE REVOLT

THE reference in the last sentence of the previous chapter is to a possible bombardment of Johannesburg. There are some who think that there was little likelihood of any disaster befalling the town, and that if the High Commissioner had taken up a high tone and "bluffed" the matter out, the Boers would have given in. These think that the Boers would never have dared to attack a great town like Johannesburg, in which they believed there were quite 20,000 rifles and Maxims and guns; that they would merely have surrounded the place, and meanwhile help could have come to the town from outside, and forced the Boers to grant reasonable concessions to the Uitlanders. Those who reason so are, I think, scarcely aware of the temper of the Boers at that time. The Boer is a very difficult gentleman to move under ordinary circumstances. He is as stubborn and stolid as the most bigoted country farmer at home. But once let the question of his independence be raised and he is all fire and vehemence in an instant. The Boers were now thoroughly convinced that their independence *was* at stake, and they were moreover highly elated at their victory over Jameson and the capture of all his war material. Whoever therefore thinks that the three thousand armed miners of Johannesburg, with *no* artillery to reply to the artillery fire which the Boers could have poured upon the town, could have held their own against the eight or ten thousand Boers who surrounded the town, seems to me to under-estimate the real position as grossly as Dr. Jameson himself did when he thought that he could successfully invade the Transvaal with less than 500 men at his back.

The line which Sir Hercules Robinson took was to persuade the Johannesburgers to lay down their arms. The British Agent, Sir Jacobus de Wet, was accordingly sent to Johannesburg on the morning of January 7th to inform the people that if they would lay down their arms the High Commissioner would consider that they were acting honourably ; but that if they refused to comply with this request they would forfeit the sympathy of the British Government and of British subjects throughout the world, as the lives of Dr. Jameson and his men were practically in their hands. This is, indeed, what was generally considered to be the case. The common rumour was that if Johannesburg continued the fighting which had begun, the Boers already highly incensed and with difficulty kept within reasonable bounds by their strong President, would carry out the decision at which the Commandant had already arrived, and simply shoot Dr. Jameson and his officers. And there was a high probability that such might now happen if the Johannesburg leaders chose to be obdurate.

Fortunately these latter thoroughly realised the gravity of the situation. They saw the impossibility of continuing a struggle which had been forced upon them, and for which they had in no way been prepared. The difficulty of bringing about a surrender of the arms lay not with the leaders but with the men who held the arms. It is often difficult to kindle a fire, but it is still more difficult to put it out once it is kindled. The Johannesburg leaders had had much trouble at first in firing the mob with any enthusiasm for revolt; now their principal anxiety was how to damp down the enthusiasm that had been kindled. Mobs are not given to thinking, and these thousands of men now roving listlessly about Johannesburg, two or three thousand of them with arms in their hands, and scarcely one of them aware in the smallest degree of the strength of the Boer forces which surrounded the town, could see no possible reason why they should throw down their arms. They naturally felt capable of anything, and the only possible way of carrying disarmament into effect was to appeal to their feeling of devotion to Dr. Jameson, and make clear to them the danger in which he would lie if they were obdurate.

In the forenoon of January the 7th a huge mob assembled outside the Club to be addressed by Sir Jacobus de Wet. I stood on the verandah close beside the British Agent, and as I looked down upon the sea of faces beneath, and saw the effects of the speech upon the people, I could realise the gravity of the crisis, and how easily trouble might come on. Sir Jacobus tried to explain to them in how defenceless a state the town was, and in what danger the women and children would lie if the men refused to give up their arms, and the Boers in consequence attacked the town. But such an appeal only served to irritate the mob. They thought themselves quite equal to dealing with any number of Boers, and they did not care for the appearance of surrendering their arms from motives of fear. The appeal on that ground tended rather to increase than diminish their determination to retain them.

A far more successful appeal was made in the speech of Sir Sidney Shippard, who told them that, rom regard for themselves alone, he knew that they would not think of laying down their arms: but that others than themselves had to be considered, and the fate of brave men were in their hands; if they persisted in a determination to retain their arms, then Dr. Jameson and his brother officers would almost certainly be killed; if, on the contrary, they listened to the request of the High Commissioner, their case would be considered by him.

The mob responded more readily to this appeal; they surlily consented to lay down their arms; by the following morning most of them had been collected.

The disarmament of Johannesburg was thus completed without mishap. Arms were collected and handed over to the Government Commissioner, Government police patrolled the town, and the crisis was passed. The news gave instant relief. Both in Johannesburg and in Pretoria it had been felt that the country was on the brink of a bloody struggle; but this had, happily, been averted by the coolness and moderation of the Republican Government, and the timely and well-considered action of the High Commissioner.

So, after lasting eight days, ended an absolutely unique revolution. Two thousand men had been in arms in what is nothing but a huge mining camp—and mining camps are not usually remarkable for good order—yet not even a policeman had been knocked on the head, and not a single act of violence had been committed. One week the Government, recognising that in the town of Johannesburg they were unable to cope with the armed forces which had suddenly sprung into existence, discreetly withdrew their men. The next week Johannesburg, finding the Government stronger than it thought, with similar discretion lays down its arms. The Government had not fired one shot at a Johannesburg man, and

Johannesburg had not fired one shot against the Government. President Kruger and the Executive exhibited throughout remarkable coolness, and the stability of the Government was unmistakably displayed.

What was very noticeable was the absence of excitement in the capital, danger and victory being regarded with like equanimity by the hardy Boers. But, though the crisis was over, deep feelings on both sides had been excited which will not be allayed for years. The Boers' distrust of the Uitlanders was increased tenfold, and the sense of failure is rankling with the Uitlanders. Both alike have a deep-rooted desire in common for the existence of the State as a Republic. The simple, pastoral Boer recoils at the thought of being governed by the schemes of Uitlander speculators, and the pushing Uitlander capitalist frets at the obstacles put in the way of his enterprises by the untrained Boers. Yet both have come to the country to remain in it, and both want the government of it to be republican and free from outside control.

The arms had been taken from the men of Johannesburg, and quiet had been restored; but the leaders of the movement—the Reform Committee—were still in grave anxiety as to what action the Transvaal Government might take against them. The Boers had at first been intensely angry with Jameson for having without warning or apparent justification invaded their country. But now amongst the baggage which they had captured they had found a letter signed by the five Johannesburg leaders, calling Jameson in. The Boers of course knew nothing of the secret history of that letter—that it had only been given to Jameson to be used under certain eventualities which had never actually transpired. The Boers had simply the fact before them that here was a letter calling in Jameson, and all the time the Johannesburg leaders had been saying that they did not want him! No wonder the Boers became furious with the five leaders who had signed the letter. I was at that time going backwards and forwards between Johannesburg and Pretoria, and in an hotel at the latter place I heard a number of the Boer commandants protesting, in that lusty emphatic way these rough men have when roused, that each one of those five ought to have "a hole drilled through him." When I returned again to Johannesburg Colonel Frank Rhodes and George Farrar asked me what was the state of feeling in Pretoria in regard to them, and I had to say that the rumours of the Boer indignation against them were perfectly true, and that they ran every chance of being shot if they remained in the country. Somebody present suggested that in that case, and as they were free and could easily leave the country in disguise, the most prudent course to adopt would be to bolt at once before they were arrested.

Apparently certain death, or at least a long imprisonment, awaited them on the one hand, and on the other they might quietly withdraw, and in a few hours be out of all danger. But the two never flinched for a moment. Frank Rhodes, with that toss of his body so characteristic of him, and throwing out his legs, said that as he had gone in for the thing he was going to see it through at whatever cost. And George Farrar, with his usual tug at his moustache, similarly said that he for one was not going to run away now they were in a tight place. The other two who signed the letter—Lionel Phillips and John Hays Hammond—also determined to stay on and face the consequences, whatever they might be.

What these were very soon appeared: for suddenly, on the evening of January 9th and on the next morning, the whole of the Reform Committee were arrested and taken to Pretoria gaol. Then the four leaders in particular and the whole number were treated at first with extreme roughness. The four leaders were locked into a small cell, with only the smallest opening for a window, and from which, though one of the number was very unwell the whole night through, there was no means of retiring. The rest were huddled into small rooms, where there was barely sufficient space to lie down packed alongside each other.

Dr. Jameson and five of his officers were in the same gaol, and I had an opportunity now of

Colonel Rhodes' House, Johannesburg.

[To face page 95.

visiting them for the first time. Of the whole number Dr. Jameson himself appeared then the weakest. He seemed utterly broken and crushed, and all the officers at that time were labouring under a sense of having been deserted by the Johannesburgers. How the misapprehension can possibly have arisen in face of the repeated messages which the Johannesburg leaders despatched to Jameson urging him not to start, it is hard to say. But officers and men seem to have made perfectly certain that men were to come out from Johannesburg to help them in. Certainly while I was in the town I never heard any mention of such an intention. The whole idea of the plan, as far as I understood it from the leaders, was—not that Johannesburg should help Jameson's force to come in, but that Jameson was to help Johannesburg *in case of trouble arising;* and in discussing the situation with the leaders after Jameson had actually started, the assumption always made was that his force would be able to get in without difficulty and without assistance. So certain indeed was I made of this and so confident had I become that any serious fighting which might occur would be much more likely to take place round the town than on the line of Jameson's march, that I stayed in Johannesburg till the latest moment, and even then only rode out to witness, as I thought it would be, the triumphant entry of Jameson into the town.

The invading force had been on the frontier for weeks and months, and its leaders knew that its possible destination might be the Transvaal. They had arranged depôts of supplies along the route to Johannesburg, and had even laid out changes of horses. They were well armed with repeating rifles, Maxims and field guns. And it was presumed that when they started in the teeth of the warnings from Johannesburg they would at least be provided with guides and be independent of assistance from the town. Yet for months the raiders were proclaimed as heroes, and the Johannesburgers denounced as curs. Blundering there was on both sides, but certainly there was neither heroism nor cowardice nor disloyalty on either. If men like Colonel Rhodes, George Farrar, Lionel Phillips and John Hays Hammond ever had made agreement to go out and meet Jameson with a force to *assist* him in, they would have done it. But all they seem to have understood that they should do was to have a certain number of men to meet Jameson—not to assist him in a military way, but—to make a political demonstration of welcoming him in. They were also to send him men for the purpose of showing him the way to the precise spot where his men should encamp near Johannesburg. In all the confusion occasioned by Jameson's premature advance they were unable to carry out the first intention, and they had on the contrary to send

WIVES WAITING OUTSIDE PRETORIA JAIL, MAY 29th, 1896.

[To face page 97.

one of their number, Mr. Lace, to beg him to return instead of coming in. As Dr. Jameson was already engaged in fighting the Boers he was no longer able to withdraw. And so, through too great impetuosity, and fatal miscalculation of possible consequences on the one side, and through weakness in allowing themselves to be drawn into an enterprise for which they were not prepared on the other, that complete combination by which alone success could be achieved was missed, and the resulting collapse was as disastrous as the brilliancy of the success upon which all had so confidently counted.

It would weary my readers to recount the dreary course of events after the "Reformers" had been placed in prison. How first a few of them were let out on bail, then all except the leaders, then the leaders. How after a long investigation the actual trial took place. How all South Africa and all England was astounded at the appalling severity of the death sentence passed on the Johannesburg leaders; and how those four—Lionel Phillips, Colonel Frank Rhodes, George Farrar, and John Hays Hammond—bore that terrible and utterly unexpected sentence with a fortitude which convinced every one who saw them that they in no way deserved the term of reproach which Englishmen had been so ready to hurl upon them at first. But I may dwell for a moment on one pathetic figure, for whom no one can be so hard as not to feel some sympathy. It is that of the man who as a boy gained his cricketing colours on the playing-fields of Eton; who for years served in one of the finest cavalry regiments of the British army; who gained the Distinguished Service Order for his gallantry on Herbert Stewart's hard desert march to the relief of Gordon at Khartoum; who is the solitary survivor of Sir Gerald Portal's arduous mission to Uganda; and who, through loyalty to his younger brother, had engaged in an ill-fated scheme in which he had absolutely no personal interest, and which had now brought him, a colonel in the British army, to the prisoner's dock, to be sentenced to death in a foreign country. Even his enemies, with all their roughness, were able to speak with admiration of the dignity with which he carried himself on this awful occasion, and to say that they understood now what was meant by the term "an English gentleman." And among his own countrymen in the Transvaal who knew him at that hard time he is spoken of with a warmth of affection which but few can inspire. But what he must feel even harder than his death sentence, or the imprisonment in Pretoria gaol, or the fine of £25,000 imposed upon him, or the enforced resignation of his commission in the army and the consequent blighting of his whole career, is the persistency with which so many of his countrymen still believe that he and the other leaders were guilty of disloyalty to Dr. Jameson in not going out to meet him.

May these leaders now expect that, as the true facts of the case are known, and that it has been made clear that however much miscalculation and misunderstanding there may have been, there was no disloyalty, that deepest reproach of all upon the character of a man may be erased for ever?

CHAPTER X

THE TRANSVAAL REVISITED

BEFORE the trial took place I had returned to England. But the state of South Africa still being unsatisfactory, the *Times* asked me to go back and visit every part of it, so as to be able to report completely on the whole situation. Reports had reached England that the Boers were arming very extensively; and on my arrival in the Transvaal I found that their report was in no way exaggerated. The Boers had very nearly been caught napping at the beginning of the year, and now that they had received a start they were running to the opposite extreme, and were making warlike preparations out of all proportion to any possible need. Fortunately for them the Boers have no necessity to count the cost of any warlike measures they may take. The cry of the overburdened taxpayer groaning under the weight of military expenditure is never heard among them; for they have the bloated Uitlander close by, whom they can always bleed for whatever amount they may require. So at the same time that these quondam farmers, who, before the advent of the Uitlander, scarcely had two pennies to jingle together, were building themselves public offices such as I saw in no other town in South Africa, and were spending hundreds of thousands of pounds on preventive measures against rinderpest, orders for batteries of field guns, quick-firing guns and Maxims, and for sufficient rifles to arm every single Dutchman in South Africa, were being sent to Europe; European drill instructors and artillerymen were being imported, and forts were being constructed round Pretoria on the most approved designs. One attempt had been made to take their country from them; they were thoroughly convinced that the attempt would be renewed at some future date: so the Boers were determined to be thoroughly on the guard the second time.

Naturally all these elaborate preparations gave ground to the opinions entertained by many that the Boers intended something more than mere defence: and President Kruger was credited with ambitions as great as those of Cecil Rhodes. If Cecil Rhodes entertained the idea of a United South Africa under the British flag, President Kruger was supposed to be equally ambitious to unite it under the Dutch; and many believed that the Boers were planning a descent upon British territory, or at the very least that they meant to repudiate the London Convention and tear aside the last shred of dependence upon Great Britain.

I accordingly sought interviews with President

Kruger, General Joubert, Chief Justice Kotze and other leading men; and certainly the impression they gave me, that defence and not offence was intended, has proved a true one. My interview with Mr. Kruger was especially interesting, for he is an altogether unique individuality. In the old Puritan days there may have been men similar to him; but certainly at the present day no one like him exists, and perhaps no one of his peculiar stamp will ever appear again. I had already on my previous visit had a lengthy interview with him, when the Chief Justice had very kindly acted as interpreter. But on the present occasion I was more thoroughly grounded in the factors of the situation, and our conversation was more free and informal. Undoubtedly the principal impression given me was the rugged strength of the man. Here was one who had as a boy left the Cape Colony in the Great Trek of 1836, and spent his whole life in a struggle for independence. Personally brave and with a force of character which has bent the people who made him their leader to do his will, he has first made his country and then kept it intact from aggression. Uneducated in all else save the knowledge of human nature, he has skilfully guided his people through dangers which would have overcome most others. And if his constant reference to Biblical texts give a stranger an impression of sanctimoniousness of the Stiggins type, this may be explained by the fact that the Bible is probably the only book he has ever read, and as he reads it constantly and seeks to guide his conduct by it, quotations from it naturally come to his lips.

President Kruger cannot be numbered among the most enlightened and progressive rulers of the earth, and he has never shown indications of any feverish ambition to push his country higher up in the scale of civilisation: but he is astute, strong and firm; he has one or two fixed ideas in his mind which he never departs from, and one of these being that, whether his country is to be progressive or not, it is at any rate to be independent, his line of conduct is plain and simple. On the present occasion I told him that I had seen and heard of the preparations which were being made, and I asked him what assurances he could give me on the subject. Sitting there in his well-known attitude in an upright arm-chair, smoking a huge pipe and expectorating profusely, he thumped upon the table at his side and bellowed back his answer, that as long as his country was not attacked he would attack no one. He said his people were farmers scattered all over the country, and had no desire to undertake all the hardships of military service. If their country was invaded they willingly assembled for its defence, but they were in no way aggressively inclined. President Kruger acknowledged that his government was making considerable military preparations, but said that the Transvaal had been wantonly invaded once, and he must guard against its being similarly invaded a second time.

At the close of my interview, and as he rose to say good-bye, he again repeated to me most emphatically that I might tell people in England that unless we attacked him he would never attack us.

I am not sure that all the Boers are with their President on this point. Raids into British territory have, before now, been made by the Boers; and many of the younger men, ignorant of the real strength of England, and elated at their success against Jameson, would have liked, on any convenient pretext, to make an attack upon Natal or Kimberley. But I sincerely believe President Kruger to be too astute to countenance any movement so absurd; and his policy is evidently to doggedly persevere in strengthening his country, and, while making all the use he can of the new-comers, to keep them well at arm's-length all the time.

This was apparent from the second part of our conversation, when I asked him if he could hold out any hopes of granting the Uitlanders the franchise. He would give the franchise to all whom he could consider loyal to the State, he said. But when I asked him what he considered to be the test of loyalty to the State, he said that taking up arms in its defence must be the qualification. All those who had fought against the native chiefs and those who had joined with the burghers in opposing Jameson, would be granted the full rights of citizenship. But of the ordinary Uitlanders, and especially of the men of Johannesburg, Mr. Kruger was highly suspicious. They had on one occasion torn down the Transvaal flag, and even hooted him, he said: and a man of Kruger's stamp, with good wholesome prejudices, is not likely ever to forget that; conciliation is not a line which he would be inclined to act on, rather would it be dogged opposition and isolation. But when I referred to the fact that the members of the community who furnished about five millions sterling out of the five and a quarter millions which the revenue of the country produced, were allowed not one single word in regard to its expenditure, he simply said that they were, at any rate, free to make as much money as they pleased, and he asked me to name any people who were less heavily taxed than they were. When I showed him that the Uitlanders of the Transvaal paid about ten times as much as the people of Great Britain, he merely said that he had not heard it before; but did not make any hint, either that taxation should be lessened, or that the Uitlanders would be given any voice in the control of the expenditure of revenue raised from them.

While, therefore, we can admire the indomitable courage, the astuteness and the inflexible perseverance which President Kruger has displayed one can realise, at the same time, how exasperating to progressive enterprising men his stolid prejudiced unyielding nature must be.

But President Kruger is not the whole State. He has much influence, and is autocratic in many ways; but his will is not absolute law. He has to reckon with the Volksraad, and conform to the will of the people to some extent; so that the very prevalent idea that whatever he may wish will be done is not, in reality, a true one. President Kruger attends the sittings of the Volksraad, and takes his seat alongside the Chairman of the Raad, and from there delivers his speech like any ordinary member. Several of these sittings of the Raad I was able to attend; and though unable to understand the language in which the debates were carried on, I was able, by means of *résumé* translations given me by a friend, and by watching the movements and gestures of the members, to gather the spirit of the scene.

Seated in concentric, semicircular rows round the raised dais upon which sat the Chairman and President Kruger, the latter dressed in an old frock coat with a broad vivid green sash bound over his shoulder, were some forty or fifty rough-bearded men, sombrely dressed in black, and of very much the same type as one would see at a country vestry meeting at home, One after another would get up and speak very volubly and excitedly for five or ten minutes, each stating his opinion of the matter under debate, with great vehemence and much gesticulation and thumping of the table, but with little attempt at reasoning. At frequent intervals during the debate the Chairman himself would join in and speak equally excitedly, and still more fre-

CHURCH STREET, PRETORIA.

[To face page 107.

quently would President Kruger do so. On the first occasion upon which I visited the Raad I saw Mr. Kruger, almost before the original speaker had finished, rise and roar in his deep big voice at the meeting, and almost break the table with his violent thumps upon it. I thought that something very important must be under debate, but was told that they were merely debating whether some minor official's salary should be cut down or increased! Mr. Kruger is always emphatic upon whatever subject he speaks. But when he wishes to really enforce a point he comes round to his great stock argument that the independence of the country would be endangered if what he wishes is not agreed to. This is unfailing, but must surely now be getting a little threadbare.

The principal debate I heard in the Pretoria Volksraad was on the question of the total prohibition of liquor to natives. A Bill was to be brought in enacting that no intoxicating liquor of any kind was ever to be sold to natives in the Transvaal. This was a sufficiently sweeping measure to adopt, involving as it did the powerful interests of the liquor trade, and meaning ruin to many men who had invested sums of money in manufactories of liquor and in establishments for the sale of it. But the Boer legislators tackled it in a light-hearted manner, and passed the Bill in a few hours. They assembled after their mid-day dinner, debated vehemently for an hour and a half, then adjourned as usual for a smoke, and when they re-assembled the Chairman rose and said he did not suppose anybody had anything further to say about the matter, and they might as well proceed to vote. And so in a single afternoon was passed a measure—fortunately in this case a beneficial one—which in other countries could not have been brought through without months of discussion.

A few weeks later, the Raad with similar haste passed measures as detrimental as the above-mentioned was beneficial. Immediately following the trial of Dr. Jameson in England and his sentence to imprisonment, there had been a marked improvement in the feeling of the Boers towards the British. Whereas they had formerly believed that by some kind of underhand means he would be allowed to go free, the Boers now saw that the British courts of law acted fairly and justly. But the favourable turn of feeling was only temporary, and the Raad in a single day passed two of the most retrogressive and irritating measures—a Press Law and an Alien Expulsion Law—to be followed later by the Aliens Immigration Law. By these the President was empowered to suppress any newspaper which might be considered to contain matter dangerous to the peace of the Republic; to expel, without appeal to a court of law, any foreigner who might by act or word take any step dangerous to the public peace;

and lastly, to prohibit any person entering the country who could not be proved to be able to support himself.

These laws were certainly opposed to the Convention of London, by which it was provided that all persons other than natives conforming themselves to the laws of the Republic should have full liberty to enter, travel, and reside in any part of the Transvaal.

And while these irksome measures were being passed, no sign was made of bringing in any measures which would increase the freedom or lighten the burden of the Uitlanders. Even the much-talked-of Municipality for Johannesburg Bill was never put through. All that was done was to propose a form of municipality which would have left no power at all in the hands of the townspeople. It is true that an Industrial Commission was appointed this year to inquire into the needs of the mining industry, but there is as yet no indication that the suggestions of this Commission are to be adopted by the Government.

The situation in the Transvaal was rendered still more sombre by the dispute which arose early in the year between the High Court on the one side and the Executive and Volksraad on the other. Neither of the two latter bodies are able to understand the true independence of a court of law; and when the High Court declared they could not recognise as binding certain resolutions of the Volksraad, President Kruger bluffly intimated to the Judges that he would turn them out and find other Judges who would. Some sort of a compromise was effected for the time being, the Judges urging a revision of the Constitution, and the President apparently agreeing to it. But no settlement has yet been arrived at, and uncertainty still prevails.

The present situation in the Transvaal is therefore not satisfactory by any means. Where there is not obstruction there is incapacity or ignorance. And on either side there is want of confidence. What the future outlook is I will discuss in the concluding chapter.

CHAPTER XI

THE OUTLOOK IN THE TRANSVAAL

Political forecasts are always difficult, but in the case of a new country like the Transvaal it is especially necessary to make some attempt to forecast the future. Could the British have seen even ten years in advance, they would never have thrown so completely aside the rights which the expenditure of blood and money in the subjugation of native races in the Transvaal had given them, nor would they have been so indifferent about their influence at Delagoa Bay. These and other instances in South African history show only too clearly the loss which has followed from having no clear prevision of possible future developments; and it was in order to have the means of making an approximate forecast that I have in my preceding chapters dealt in some detail with the ground factors of the question.

The material conditions of the country were first enquired into, for upon those conditions depends the whole future of the country; and here fortunately there is little room for miscalculation. The gold may be extracted faster or slower, more cheaply or dearly, according to the political conditions which prevail. But about the presence of the gold in immense quantities there is no doubt whatever. It is known to a certainty that 700 millions of gold lie hidden in the Transvaal, and still more gold deposits are being discovered every month in the Lydenburg, Zoutpansberg, and Barberton districts. Nor is there any doubt as to the existence of coal and iron in almost inexhaustible quantities, besides silver, lead, copper, and other baser minerals. It cannot yet be said with certainty either that the coal is of sufficiently good quality for use on the fastest ocean-going steamers, or that an iron industry could be profitably established within the next year or two. But there is coal good enough for use on railways and in iron foundries, and, with cheapened rates and improvements on the railway and at the wharves, the price of coal may be reduced to a rate at which Transvaal coal might compete advantageously with Welsh, as far up as Aden, for use on the number of freight steamers trading in the Indian Ocean, even if the great passenger lines will not take it. And there is every prospect of an iron industry arising to take the place of the gold long before the latter is exhausted. Without the gold to give the first impetus, the Transvaal might never have been opened up. But the gold has brought population and capital into the country, and has caused the construction of railways throughout the Transvaal. Every other industry will therefore start with these initial advantages in its favour. The value of hens' eggs annually produced in the United States is greater than the value of the gold output. And with the many other natural resources besides gold which the Transvaal possesses, with its healthy climate and good soil, it should be obvious that prosperity will not forsake it when the gold is gone. A large permanent population, which in ten years time may be expected to reach half a million, and eventually amount to three or four millions, will settle in the country, which will become the most populous State in South Africa.

This seemingly obvious fact the Boers do not recognise. They contend that the Uitlanders only come to make money and go back to Europe, and that when the gold is all worked out there will be no Uitlanders left. Uitlanders do come to the Transvaal to make money, and few of them with any other object; but of the money they earn the greater part is kept invested in the country, and it is to the interest of every money-maker in the Transvaal that the country should be properly developed and its Government sound and strong. The Boers, then, do not realise the future that lies before the country; and their history and character show that, while they are strong and capable as rough pioneers, they have not the peculiar genius, the energy, and the imagination required for the development of so inordinately rich a country as the Transvaal. While I was much impressed with the coolness, the quiet strength, and large-heartedness of the Boers during the troublous times at the beginning of last year, I have been equally impressed during the present year with their present incapacity for dealing with a young and rising State. I think, therefore, that the Uitlanders for some years yet need not hope to see in the Transvaal the kind of government which they as men of the nineteenth century have a right to expect, and which so magnificent a country deserves. They will have to anticipate constant friction and disappointment—not, I would repeat, from any deliberate intention on the part of the Boers to crush the mining industry, but from their ignorance of what rough handling of so delicate an organism means. The class of Boer who now sit in the Volksraad have no idea of what the effect of measures they so hastily pass really will be; they do not understand that the hint of such a measure as the stopping of the automatically-running stamps on Sundays has much the same effect on the industry as the touch of the hand on the sensitive plant. And if both Boers and Uitlanders were always to remain the same as they are to-day, a revival of the troubles of the beginning of last year might certainly be expected.

The hope, however, that this will not be the case arises from the reflection that the stolid Boer character is slowly changing in the new surroundings of the people and under the constant pressure now bearing on them. The old isolation so hardly sought after is no longer possible. The Boers are hemmed in, and the flood of civilisation is upon them. The young Boer has not the same prejudice as his father for living all his life on a solitary farm; he likes to come in at times and see something of life in towns. More significant still, the young Boer girls do what they can to improve their education, and are always glad to marry Englishmen. Railways now traverse the country in every direction. The Boers are seeing more of the world, and those who have come most in contact with other Europeans most realise the necessities for progress. Such progress is more possible among the Boers than at first appears likely, because they are few in numbers, and because they are not an ancient people who have lived for centuries in the same country, building institutions and traditions, and forming classes in a rigid, unadaptable society. Their character is stiff, but not so stiff as that of the typical Scotchman, whom in many ways they resemble; and as their Constitution is not half a century old, and they have no hereditary ruler or privileged classes with vested interests to retard progress, they may, under the immense pressure bearing upon them from every side, be carried along faster than is generally anticipated. President Kruger is the chief obstacle to progress at present, and it is natural that a man with a history like his, who was among the original fore-trekkers who left the Cape Colony sixty years ago, and who through all his life from that time to the present year has been engaged in a struggle for independence, should at the close of his career strive to avoid a change from the system he has been so long accustomed to. But Mr. Kruger cannot remain in power for more than a few years longer, and his influence in any case wanes when there is no pressure from outside to bind the people together under him as a military leader. At the end of 1895 there was a feeling even among the Boers of the Transvaal that he was not acting either fairly or prudently towards the Uitlanders, but was driving them to rebellion; and the Dutch of Cape Colony and the Free States were incensed against him because of the heavy duties he imposed upon colonial produce, and because he employed Hollanders in the Government offices instead of Dutchmen trained in the colony. The events of the beginning of last year for the time alienated all this sympathy; but of the two most likely successors to the Presidency one has said to me that he looked to the time when all South African States would meet together for the settlement of matters of mutual interest; and the other told me that, having regard to the increasing number of the Uitlanders who were coming into the country, he saw that the present block system could not long continue, and that a beginning must be made towards letting Uitlanders acquire the rights of citizenship in the country of their adoption.

At the same time the Uitlanders are certain, as the ill-feeling raised by the raid subsides, to gain an increased influence in the State. The first feverish rush to the gold fields is over, and a better class of men will come to the country, while men of standing and influence will be sent out from England to represent the great financial houses. And the parties into which the Boers must divide will find that, both in their own interest and in that of their country, it will be necessary to have the support of these men. The rinderpest, again, may prove a very efficient cause of increasing Uitlander influence. The disease is bound to spread through the whole country. Already over 60,000 head of cattle have been carried off, and half the Boers are absolutely dependent on cattle for their livelihood. An amount of money four times as great as the total revenue of the country before the Uitlanders came has already been budgeted for rinderpest expenses; and the Boers will now be placed in the position of either having to go to the Uitlanders for a far larger sum as compensation for the cattle losses or of setting really to work.

By waiting on their opportunity the Uitlanders will gradually gain their end. Their lot is not a desperate one. They run no immediate risk of being exterminated like Armenians; and instead of hastily resorting to arms and reviving racial feeling, which impedes progress, they can well afford to wait a few years time till the Boers, not bound together in opposition as they are now through being attacked, have spread themselves out, and left interstices between them by means of which the process of a new amalgamation may be carried out.

A curious anomaly in the situation is that the British subjects in the Transvaal consider they may justly demand assistance from the British Government to enable them to become independent Republicans. But, if this may be considered a too excessive demand, they have, at any rate, the right to expect that England will see that the Boers will faithfully carry out their treaty engagements. The Boers for years have shown an inclination to whittle away the London Convention—the present Convention, it will be remembered, having already been largely modified from the original. And England has a special right to insist that her subjects, while they remain her subjects, should be treated with common fairness, if she cannot expect for them the liberality with which she treats the subjects of other countries in her own colonies. The Boers will not allow that they owe England any debt of gratitude for saving them from total disintegration twenty years ago, when they had only 12*s.* 6*d.* left in their treasury, because England so mismanaged them afterwards when she took over the country. But they must admit that while they themselves have borne, perhaps, the greater share in clearing the country and rendering it secure for settlement, the British also have taken no small part, for it was a British army which defeated Sikukuni, and it was a British army which broke the power of the Zulus. Gratitude is not to be expected between nations, but each has to see that it is used with justice by the other. When England restored the Transvaal to the Boers she stipulated for fair treatment of her subjects. That stipulation has barely been fulfilled in the letter, much less in the spirit; and there are further very good grounds for believing that attempts to secure an alliance with Germany as a counterpoise to British influence have been made, while it is certain that for many years past Germany has been endeavouring to establish a footing and spread her influence in South Africa. England, as the Power responsible for the peace of by far the greater portion of South Africa—of countries populated by as many Dutchmen as Englishmen—cannot afford to see her subjects in the Transvaal treated in such a manner as would cause disaffection likely to spread in racial strife throughout South Africa. Still less can she afford to see another European Power settling as a rival there. Neither, therefore, could the Transvaal be allowed to extend its territories towards the coast beyond the limits carefully defined in the Convention which restored the country to the Boers; nor could the Germans be permitted to gain the footing they are believed to be seeking in Delagoa Bay. This much England in her own interests has need to look after. She must keep at a distance all rivals to the supremacy she has fought and worked for in South Africa, and she must see so far as is possible that no favour is shown to others over her own subjects.

Provided she does this—provided she sees her

subjects have fair play—the Uitlanders in the Transvaal may well be left to work out their own salvation in their own way. The British portion need expect no encouragement from the Boers, and they may indeed expect that the Government, in any quiet way it can, will favour Germans, French, and Hollanders with the object of lessening the preponderance of British influence and of driving away British capital, to see it replaced by German and French. But British investors, manufacturers, and settlers will always remember the immense future possibilities of the country, and persevere in their work of developing its wonderful resources. And every European nation equally with England should be interested in seeing that no unnecessary hindrance is placed in the way of its development, and should bring all the force of public opinion to bear upon the Boers to make them realise that at this stage of the world's history a mere handful of men cannot be permitted to obstruct the progress of a country so valuable to overcrowded Europe as is the Transvaal.

The eventual product of this development is likely to be a State the majority of whose inhabitants will be British by birth, but Republican in their ideas and inclinations. Whether this, the most rich and populous of the South African States of the future, will preponderate over the rest will depend upon whether the Transvaal or Great Britain controls the outlet to the sea.

CHAPTER XII

RHODESIA

FROM the Transvaal, in company with Mr. Harry Cust, I proceeded to Rhodesia, and after travelling through Mashonaland reached Bulawayo just as the Matabele campaign had been brought to a conclusion.

Even to a greater degree than the remainder of South Africa, Rhodesia is a country of surprises, contrasts, and rapid changes. Three years ago the site of Bulawayo was the headquarters of a barbarian king. Now, the traveller rides through streets of English shops, business offices, and residential chambers to an hotel where all ordinary European luxuries can be obtained. He finds a tidy, well-kept club, with English newspapers scarcely a month old, and local papers containing telegraphic news from England of the previous day. A few short months before my visit the town was surrounded by thousands of wolfish savages thirsting for the blood of their European conquerors, and reeking with that of hundreds of their defenceless victims cruelly murdered on their solitary farms and wayside stores; while, in the town itself, the streets were thronged with Englishmen hastily armed and organised to defend their new-found homes, and sternly resolved to exact a terrible revenge on those who had murdered their wives and children, their brothers, and their friends. Now these self-same streets were filled with crowds of starving natives, seeking and obtaining food from the very men they had attempted to exterminate. In the hall of the Stock Exchange eighty-five of these uncouth barbarian chiefs of the country were squatting on the floor discussing with Captain Lawley, the company's representative, the boundaries of the districts in future to be allotted to them, while the white men, discarding their arms again, had returned to their business offices. The leader in one of the most successful fights was engaged in ordering up armchairs and fresh consignments of champagne and cigars for the club. Another equally successful leader was organising parties to prospect for further gold, and ordering machinery for the mines already started before the outbreak. Everywhere was change, everything was new, and even the very natives of the country have no old history, no old traditions—nothing to fix them down for more than half a century. Neither in Europe nor Asia, nor even, perhaps, in America, could a similar country be found. A single photograph of such a country is therefore of but little use. To appreciate its aspects at all we must employ the Edisonian system of moving pictures, in order that the living, throbbing scene may produce a true impression on the mind.

It would be necessary that the series of pictures, which, thrown on the screen in rapid succession, would form one living whole, should commence at the time when all Rhodesia was inhabited by conglomerates of savage tribes living in constant fear of one another, but leading on the whole a careless, easy existence, the men compelling their women folk to do all the labour, to scratch up the soil in little patches round their kraals on which to grow corn sufficient for their meagre needs. Such a picture would show a country of rolling grassy downs, and hill and dale, of meadow land and forests with richly-tinted trees of every graceful form, and the greater part of this rich land would be seen left to the teeming herds of game and troops of lions and other beasts of prey, while the natives occupied only secluded corners in it. The series would then go on to show the Zulu invasion from the south, the formation of the Matabele nation, and the new comers amalgamating with the old under the strong, even rule of Lobengula. It would show the advent of the white man, the hunters, traders, and missionaries, and, lastly, the concession seekers, who, noting the many signs of the presence of gold, the richness of the valleys, and the mildness of the climate, sought to gain access to the country to work it for their benefit. No picture could show the feelings which actuated these men, the belief of some few leaders that they were advancing the interests of their own native country in the great struggle of the nations of the earth, the belief of the many that they would be enabled here to provide themselves with a livelihood more quickly and more easily than in their overcrowded native land. But the picture would go on to show these white men now coming into the country in a combined body, struggling against every hardship, against possible attack from natives, against fever, pestilence, and starvation, and all the many obstacles to the first settlement of a strange people in a new country. It would show many dying from privations, many returning discouraged, but others coming in their places, and the whole gradually spreading themselves over the land and consolidating their power in it. Then small towns and settlements would be seen springing up; small parties of gold seekers threading through the land like ants in every direction, and shafts of mines being sunk in favourable localities, while long strings of waggons would be seen leaving their tracks upon the land and wearing out roads from one end of the country to the other.

The living pictures would rapidly move across the screen till the scene of conflict between the black inhabitants and the white invaders would be reached. At first would be observed a small conflict between a few blacks and whites, and then two columns of whites, converging from north and south, advancing boldly into the very midst of the half of the country still ruled by a native chief, fighting ten times the number of blacks; but in spite of all the risks they ran, of annihilation by weight of overwhelming numbers, of starvation, and of exposure, defeating the native chief and all his force till they drove him from the country and annexed it for themselves. The whites are now spread over the whole country. On the very spot where the old native chief held his court the new white ruler builds his house. Now white settlements spring up, strings of waggons come into the country, the thin lines of telegraph run right through it, prospectors for gold in knots of twos and threes spread over the land, gold mines are sunk and dotted over each district, along every road, and wherever a small mining community is formed, stores for the sale of liquor, food, and goods are erected. The natives, stunned by the suddenness and force of the blow dealt to them, appear to have accepted the inevitable; they allow the white man to settle on their lands, they allow him to carry them off to labour in the mines, they appear, indeed, to have submitted so meekly that the whites withdraw all their armed forces; and the lonely prospectors, the solitary stores, the distant farmhouses are left at the mercy of the black inhabitants in fancied security.

But now comes the crash. The black man has

only been stunned; he has not been beaten. He sees his whilom conqueror defenceless, and he turns upon him before he can arm. And through all the land the natives are seen murdering the white men, their women and their children, burning down their stores and homesteads, and destroying everything they possess. The land is black once more, all except a few white spots still left upon it. But those white spots remain untouched by the seething tide of black around them till other white columns come streaming into the country, till the flood is yet again turned, and the blacks are thrown back for ever.

Such a complete series of living scenes I cannot pretend to give in detail, I can only show with fidelity the last in the series—the aspect of Rhodesia at the present time. As I entered the country at its northern end from the sea coast at Beira, signs of progress were already visible. The Portuguese town of Beira was rapidly becoming an English settlement in appearance. Nearly all the shops were English; the hotels were English; even the telegraph office was English, and English companies were building piers in the fine harbour, and constructing the line of railway to Salisbury which is already completed to Massi Kessi, and which is expected to reach its destination by the middle of next year. Instead of having to trudge through the pestilential swamps of the low country, weakened by the inevitable fever and stricken

View near Massi Kessi.

[To face page 126.

down by the tropical sun, as the pioneers of a few years since were obliged to do, I was able to reach the cool and healthy highlands of the interior by train, and, crossing the Portuguese border, arrived at the first town in the Chartered Company's territory at Umtali. A newly-formed frontier town in South Africa is not a lovely object. The surroundings of Umtali were as beautiful as rugged hill and dale and varied coloured forest could make them, and the picturesqueness of the sight was increased at the time of my visit by the richness of the spring foliage, which here in Africa, instead of being uniformly green, has all the varied hues of an English autumn—its bright reds and yellows, and deep claret-coloured tints intensified to a degree only equalled in Kashmir. But the town itself was as unlovely as its site was beautiful. Pioneers have little time or inclination to indulge the æsthetic side of their natures. They lay out the towns in long straight streets, crossing each other at strict right angles; they erect along these streets the useful but hideous sheds of corrugated iron; they leave a huge dust-trap in the middle, where all the dust collects from whichever quarter the wind may blow, and then call it the market square. A town has arisen upon the face of the earth, and though its population may be only that of a little village at home it is henceforth marked in large letters on every map, and its inhabitants are amazed at the ignorance of the English when on reaching home again they find that the people there have never heard of such a place.

And here at Umtali I received that first impression of the "localism" which is so characteristic a feature of the settlers in Rhodesia. Every inhabitant of Umtali has unbounded confidence in the future of his town. It is not much to look at in the present; but you have only to think of what it will become—just to go out and see the gold mines which are being started all round, and the splendid agricultural possibilities of the district. Upon such a promising town the Administration ought, in the opinion of the man of Umtali, to spend all their energies first; and if he thinks that more attention is being paid to some other town he fumes and grumbles, and writes petitions to Government and letters to the newspapers till, by dint of sheer hard grumbling, he has induced the Company to press forward the railway a little quicker towards his locality. The same feature was noticeable in Salisbury, in Victoria, in Gwelo, in Bulawayo—wherever I went. Each town was jealous of the other, and all were confident of their future. Like the French soldier who believes that one day he may obtain the Field-Marshal's bâton, each town in Rhodesia believes in the possibilities of its turning out a second Johannesburg, and does its best to make it one. This localism is the soul of success; and it will be through this, if at all, that Rhodesia

Cape Cart en route to Salisbury.

[To face page 129.

will become the magnificent country its present inhabitants believe it is likely to develop into in the future.

Up to Umtali, with the arrangements which Colonel Beale, the skilled leader of the column which brought relief from Salisbury to Bulawayo, and afterwards back again from Bulawayo to Salisbury, had made for Mr. Cust and myself, we were able to travel without risk. Beyond that the country was still unsafe, and military operations were not yet concluded. And, as we now began to come in contact with the men who had fought so strenuously for their adopted country and for the welfare of the Empire, as we saw the positions they had had to attack, and passed by the ashy ruins of the wayside inns and once flourishing farmhouses where English women and children had been so cruelly butchered, we were able to realise something of the nature of the war then scarcely concluded, to ascertain its causes and appreciate its results.

Had the natives been sufficiently subdued to prevent a second rising, or were they merely taking breathing space to recoup their strength before having one more struggle for freedom? Men who were rightly looked upon as the best acquainted with the native mind say that, after many years' residence in the country, they feel still so ignorant of the nature of the people as to be unable to predict what they may do next. But the nature of the black inhabitants of Rhodesia does not appear to be very greatly different from that of barbarous races all the world over; or from that of children in civilised races. All alike are impulsive, and find difficulty in resisting temptation. Withdraw the sign of authority and they are mischievous—and mischief with such people means cruelty. Keep authority in evidence, and use it tactfully, and they behave themselves. But, in the case of Rhodesia, all signs of an authority which had never been thoroughly established was withdrawn; and the people, not having been tactfully and sympathetically, but, on the contrary, harshly and roughly treated, rose in revolt. They saw their would-be rulers with their means of authority thrown away; and they saw many of those who had treated them more as brute beasts than human beings lying defenceless in their power. Little wonder, therefore, that they were unable to restrain their impulses or resist the temptation. What is remarkable is that they were able to combine as they did, for they had no recognised chief to rally round, and they had no religious enthusiasm to bind them together. Under ordinary circumstances they probably never would have combined. But, at the beginning of last year, so much occurred to bring matters to a focus all at once that they were forced to combine in a way they might never otherwise have done. As a sequel to the visitation of locusts, which till the arrival of the white man were unknown in this part of Africa, and just after the police had been withdrawn from the country, came the rinderpest. The climax of irritation (for locusts and rinderpests were alike put down to the whites) and the climax of opportunity were both reached at the same time.

The result was an outbreak of brutal savagery never before equalled in South African history. There was no warning. No attempt was made to take captives, and no quarter was given. Suddenly, wherever white men or women could be found in isolated positions away from the towns, they were cruelly murdered and their bodies most horribly mutilated.

As news of these frightful atrocities reached the towns, as men who had had hairbreadth escapes arrived to tell the tale, and as the people realised their precarious position, the wildest panic often occurred, and men rushed frantically to the stores for arms and ammunition, of which there was an insufficient quantity. Women were hastily assembled together in the most defensible buildings. At Bulawayo three poor women were prematurely confined in the rooms of the club. Then, when the settlers had time to organise themselves for defence and to send out patrols to relieve out-stations, and when they came across the mutilated corpses of their friends and, worse still, of women and children, and saw the burning ruins of their homesteads, it is not to be wondered at that they gave no quarter to any native. The whites were engaged in a life-and-death struggle with a savage foe utterly reckless of human life. The fiercest feelings on either side were aroused, and deeds of vengeance were committed which few would feel inclined to dwell upon now in the after-calm.

A far more pleasing task is to record some of the many instances of devoted heroism which this struggle brought forth. The rough prospectors in Rhodesia were as good friends as they were bad enemies, and one of the most remarkable features of the war was the manner in which the settlers stood by one another. There was the case of a man named Edwards, who had walked for fifty-two miles through the bush in one day to escape from the natives, but who, directly he arrived in Bulawayo, collected a few men together and set out to relieve a friend. There was the case of Windley, who saved Mr. Selous's life by carrying him away on his horse when the natives were all around him. There was the telegraphist Blakiston, who, in sight of the rebels, walked for over a mile from the laager to the telegraph station to send off a warning telegram to Salisbury, though he knew full well that he would never be allowed to return alive by the natives, who did in fact cruelly murder him. And many other instances besides these might be quoted of individual heroism apart from the noble efforts made by relief patrols to succour their friends in outlying stations. There is no more brilliant example than the relief of the Alice Mine, twenty-seven miles from Salisbury, when six men and three women were surrounded in an open laager by hundreds of natives, who could fire directly down upon them, and who were relieved by two small patrols of a dozen men each under Nesbitt and Judson, and carried away in a hastily armoured waggon in broad daylight through the midst of the rebel hordes hidden in the long grass and among the rocky kopjes by the road. Such cases as these, and others in which leaders like Spreckley, Van Niekerk, George Grey, and Maurice Gifford brought their men through many a hard struggle with the natives, showed the true self-reliant and resolute character of the settlers.

But it was not the settlers alone who pacified Rhodesia, and too little credit has been given to the part which Imperial officers and troops took in the war. Every one in Bulawayo spoke in admiration of the behaviour of Captain Nicholson, of the 7th Hussars, in the first stern days of the outbreak at Bulawayo; and there was no leader more successful in the fight, and under whom the men would more readily rally than Captain Macfarlan, an ex-officer of the 9th Lancers. The conduct of Colonel Plumer, who hastily raised a volunteer force in Cape Colony and marched them up for hundreds of miles to the relief of Matabeleland, organising and drilling his men as he went along, and subsequently fighting some of the most decisive actions in the campaign, was such as to give those who saw and appreciated the nature of his work the impression that a brilliant future was before him. Colonel Baden-Powell earned a reputation for restless activity even among the natives, and his own countrymen appreciated to an equal degree his cool-headedness, common-sense, and resourcefulness. And the services of Colonel Bridgman in organising something approaching to a transport and supply department were highly appreciated. The 7th Hussars were handicapped for many reasons, the chief of which was their arrival upon the scene of action when the enemy had retired into their rocky kopjes, and when, in consequence, the time for useful action by cavalry had passed. They only on one or two occasions had the opportunity of using their swords effectually, but they were able to establish a reputation for efficiency in rifle practice which few expected cavalry soldiers to possess. The Mounted Infantry were more fortunate, arriving in Mashonaland just when they were most wanted. Imperial troops have not a good name in South Africa. The raiders who marched to Doornkop are heroes, but Thomas Atkins finds little favour. It was refreshing, therefore, to hear the praises bestowed on Colonel Alderson for the skill with which he planned an attack on Makoni's stronghold by a sudden *détour* at night from his apparent line of march, and for the bravery with which his troops stormed a position honeycombed with caves and much more adapted for the operations of ferrets than of soldiers. This, the first, and many other operations which the

Mounted Infantry had to conduct, sometimes under Colonel Alderson in person, sometimes under Major Jenner, an officer who gained the especial confidence of the settlers for his coolness and skill, and sometimes under Captain Macmahon and junior officers, led to the restoration of order in Mashonaland, and, what to some will be equally gratifying, the restoration in some measure of the prestige of the British soldier. Even Dutchmen acknowledged that these Mounted Infantry could shoot, and were astonished at the precision of the volleys which they poured in on the enemy's positions. The operations which these Imperial troops, Hussars as well as Mounted Infantry, had to undertake were conducted under conditions the trying nature of which may be appreciated by the fact that out of twelve officers and 150 men, seven officers and seventy-six men were at one time in hospital. The operations covered a period of several months, during the whole of which the troops had to march without tents, with little transport, with inadequate supplies, and with horses falling out from sheer impoverishment. And they had to fight an enemy retired into hills of gigantic granite boulders, belched forth from the bowels of the earth apparently for the only useful purpose of hiding blacks between their crevices and interstices.

That General Sir Frederic Carrington under these circumstances, with only a few hundred Imperial troops, a few more hundreds hastily-raised levies and Cape natives, and with his base practically at Cape Town, could bring off no single conspicuous action was not surprising. To clear such a nest of strongholds as the Matoppos, nearly forty miles in length and from ten to twenty miles broad, at least 5,000 men would have been required, and these there was no possibility of feeding. The campaign therefore resolved itself into a long series of small engagements chiefly noticeable for the devoted bravery of officers like Major Kershaw and Captain Haynes, who, though they lost their lives in doing so, led their men dauntlessly on to the very mouth of the horrible caves in which the enemy secreted themselves.

The results of the war were not so decisive as might have been wished. It would have been more satisfactory and conclusive to have had one decisive action, in place of the numerous little engagements into which the campaign devolved. The loss to the natives would probably have been less, but the moral effect of a concentrated blow would have been far greater and more lasting. Once, however, the natives had retired to their rocky fortresses there was no possibility of bringing on such an engagement. Yet it must not be imagined that because there has been no single big fight the results of the war are altogether indecisive. The natives certainly had the satisfaction of murdering large numbers of whites at the commencement of the outbreak, but the numbers they themselves lost were nearly ten times as great Hundreds of their villages were burnt. Their flocks and herds were captured and their grain stores carried off or destroyed. As a practical result of their uprising they found themselves on the verge of starvation—they found the military strength of the whites considerably increased and forts established in their midst, and before the year is out they will see the iron railroad run right into the heart of the country. At the same time they find the whites inclined to treat them more reasonably and considerately than they have hitherto done; and they have had ample opportunity of airing their grievances to the great white chief Rhodes, who exercises by his personality such a wonderful influence over them, and they have received practical assurance from the Government that those grievances have been considered.

The probability of a further general rising seems, therefore, very remote. Combination is always effected with difficulty among such tribes, and was only carried out last year under very exceptional circumstances. Each chief is extremely jealous of the other, and the divisions among them have been increased through some of the chiefs having remained friendly during the recent troubles, instead of joining the majority. The war brought no one chief prominently to the front, and the people remain as loose and disconnected as before. While, then, purely local disturbances, such as occurred lately in British Bechuanaland, and occasional murders of white men, such as are committed every year upon the Indian frontier, may be expected, there is no reason to suppose that, with the police force now established in the country and with the improved system of native administration now being introduced, there will be another general rising. Other results of the war are the confirming among Rhodesians of a strong feeling of clanship, and of unbounded confidence in Mr. Rhodes as a man of courage, who stood alongside them in the midst of dangers and skilfully guided the country through a terrible crisis. The strongest incentive has been given to railway development. And lastly, the authorities have been made to recognise the necessity of regarding the interests of the natives as inseparable from the interests of the country.

CHAPTER XIII

THE OUTLOOK IN RHODESIA

RHODESIA is a country with no past, it is essentially a country of the future. Every one there lives in the future. The people talk of what this or that place will be, not what it is; and of what such and such a company will do, not what they are doing. The settlers must necessarily be imaginative, must look ahead and attempt to define the future. But at the bottom of all speculation as to the future they must have some groundwork of fact in the present; and it is this ground for their speculation that it is essential to examine.

What every one counts on to start the country is, of course, gold. To make the country a permanently prosperous colony there must be agricultural resources to back up this gold. But agriculture alone could never start the country, or make it anything more than a useful place of refuge for the restless Boers who find the Transvaal already too crowded for them. It was, therefore, into the possibilities of gold-mining development that I directed my first inquiries in my tour through the country; and if I cannot record having heard of any large output of gold at present, I can at any rate say that wherever I went I saw signs of the precious metal. Round Umtali, round Salisbury, Victoria, Gwelo, Bulawayo, Tati, in the neighbourhood of each town I visited, I saw or heard of gold mines present and prospective.

And the extensive area over which gold has been found is one of the strongest arguments in favour of gold mining becoming a permanent industry. No one has a right to expect a second industry such as that of Johannesburg to arise in Rhodesia. That may come eventually, of course; but till now only quartz reefs, whose chief characteristic is the irregularity of the occurrence of gold, have been found, and the mining must consequently be very speculative. Nor, so far, have any great results been obtained, the total output since the first commencement being under 6,000 ounces—that is, a value of about £20,000. But shafts have been sunk, and more than surface evidence has been afforded to judge of the possibilities of the reefs. And it must be remembered that the cost of bringing up machinery for the working of the mines has hitherto been prohibitive. What that cost is may be judged when I say that a bank manager who wished to have up a safe into Mashonaland, found that it would cost him £100 in carriage. Mining companies are awaiting the

TREKKING IN MASHONALAND.

[*To face page 140.*

advent of the railway; and till that comes, till they can import their machinery at a reasonable rate, and practically prove by actual working the value of some of the principal reefs, no definite opinion can be formed as to the future of the mining industry. It is a matter of hope and expectation. But it is worth recording that the settlers themselves have the utmost faith in it, and the value of land in the townships at each of the mining centres remains exorbitantly high, in spite of all the troubles of the year.

In the matter of necessary accessories to a gold-mining industry—labour, water, fuel, climate—Rhodesia is, too, fairly well provided. The present native labour is not good, and the system hitherto employed in gaining it has been hateful. Natives who had no inclination to work—who were unaccustomed to work even in their fields—were hunted out to work in mines, and not always well or justly treated there. Such a system could never last, and the unwilling labour thus obtained, in the long run, was the most expensive that could be found. For a few years some kind of pressure will be necessary to make natives work; and as long as the Government see that the men so employed are properly treated, they will probably be all the better for a little lesson in the "dignity of labour." But with the arrival of railways from the north and south other labour markets will be made available, and men may be expected to come and work as readily as they do in Johannesburg and Kimberley. Then, again, water is generally obtainable and in most places plentiful. There may be difficulty in regard to the supply of coal till the railways are built, but it has been found near Salisbury, about sixty miles to the west of Bulawayo, and again quite lately in Bechuanaland.

The climate on the elevated plateaux is cool and healthy, though the low country is feverish. Many deaths have occurred and many have been stricken down by fever; but this is not due to any inherent unhealthiness in the climate of the uplands, but to the fact that all the first arrivals had to reach the country by many weeks of travel through the pestilential low country, and even on their reaching the uplands had only poor and scanty fare and had to live a hard rough life, with no proper houses to dwell in. What is locally known as "whisky fever" is also accountable for much. The lower valleys will always remain feverish. But the climate of towns like Salisbury and Bulawayo is as good as that of any town in South Africa. The summer heat is very little greater than that of England, and in the winter there are mild frosts.

Agriculture in Rhodesia must depend on the development of the gold-mining industry. The country seems to have all the requisites for a rich agricultural colony, and in Mashonaland especially there are rich, well-watered valleys where anything might be grown, and there are thousands of acres

HOTEL, MASHONALAND.

[To face page 142.

of sweet good grass for sheep and cattle. One beautiful glen, which a knowing Boer farmer had appropriated, I particularly recall to remembrance. It might have been taken out of Surrey. Low, rich meadow lands, with a clear little stream meandering through it, and the hills on either side covered with shady copses. Yet while one sees all this and hears the favourable opinions of men who have had experience in other parts of South Africa one cannot help recalling also the many drawbacks to agriculture which are so apparent at the same time. Why are the natives starving in parts where the war did not reach? Because of the drought. Why do they fear for the new crops? Because of the locusts. Why are cattle, horses, and mules, sheep and fowls so dear? Because of the rinderpest, horse sickness, sheep sickness, fowl sickness. Every animal seems to have an especial sickness prescribed for it, and the drawbacks to the development of agriculture are so great that without the gold industry to first open out the country and afterwards to supply a local market, little might be expected. But the gold has already brought railways and some population into the country, and a few of the settlers who have strength to stand out against the all-absorbing attraction of gold mining or prospecting are trying their fortune at agriculture. Proposals have been made by Mr. Grafton, of Natal, and others, to establish experimental farms; and Lord Grey is giving all the attention he can spare to agricultural developments. Mr. Rhodes, too, has a personal enthusiasm for everything pertaining to the soil, and has done much to encourage good farmers by gifts of merino sheep, and grants of land on easy terms. Companies with plenty of capital who are able to farm on a large scale and tide over temporary misfortunes which would swamp small farmers are being formed.

While, then, one cannot at present see in Rhodesia all the magnificent prospects of the Transvaal, there is much to justify the transparent faith of the settlers in its future. They know that only a portion of the immense tracts of land on either side of the Zambesi known as Rhodesia has so far been touched, and that even this portion has been but roughly prospected over; yet the results of this prospecting have been sufficiently encouraging to warrant the expenditure of large sums of money in the construction of railways. Railways, again, will facilitate mining, and mining will render agriculture commercially possible. A steady development of the country for some years to come may therefore be certainly expected.

By whom and how should the country be governed in future? This was the question which was much exercising the minds of settlers in Rhodesia, and upon the question the settlers have no two minds. Imperial rule is hated; rule by the Company is appreciated. The settlers say that Imperial administration is too slow-moving for the needs of a young colony. There is too much red tape about it ; London is distant, and men at the head of affairs there are disposed to interfere for the purpose of satisfying faddists in Parliament or to pacify the Exeter Hall party, which Rhodesians imagine has such a controlling effect upon the affairs of the Empire. The Colonial Office is supposed to be ignorant of the needs and conditions of the country, and too much swayed by ill-informed public opinion in England. Any sort of interference from home is hotly resented by the sensitive colonists, and direct Imperial administration would be in the last degree distasteful to them.

Company rule is by no means held by them as a pattern of perfection. The general complaints against it, indeed, are often only a degree less fervid than the agitation against the Boers at Johannesburg. Some of the articles in the Salisbury papers before the arrival of Mr. Rhodes compared not unfavourably with articles in Johannesburg papers at the commencement of last year. The favouritism, the advantages given to men who may have influence in England, are often bitterly complained of by hardworking settlers. The *personnel* of the administration is recognised to be inefficient. Settlers are well aware of the number of incompetent and often dishonest officials there have been in the Company's service. They see how the Company is defrauded on every side.

They know that the native administration has been grossly misconducted in the past, and they complain bitterly of the injustice done to themselves in withdrawing all police protection for a raid on the Transvaal.

Yet, in spite of these recognised shortcomings, and in spite of their loudly-expressed complaints, they prefer Chartered Company rule to direct Imperial administration. Much is talked at home of these colonists being pioneers of Empire, but out there one hears very little of Imperialism. The men who come out do not come for the purpose of extending the Empire. The Empire is one of the last things they think of, though they would all join in heart and soul to assist England if she were ever in distress. But what they do come for is to make a living. The guiding minds who direct the schemes of colonisation may, or may not, have the extension and welfare of the Empire as their ideal; but the ordinary colonist settles in Rhodesia either because he thinks he can make money more rapidly there than elsewhere, or because he wants to lead a free, unfettered style of life. One class wants a Government which, good or bad, will at any rate push ahead, and the other class desires to be left alone as much as possible. All alike have faith in themselves and in the future of the country; and they believe that the pushing Chartered Company, spirited and generous as it has always shown

CECIL J. RHODES. [*To face page* 147.

From a photograph by Russell & Sons.

itself, can do more for them than the slow and righteous Imperial Government ever would. Under the one, development will be rapid, if not solid; under the other, it may be solid, but it will not be rapid. With the Chartered Company money will be made more quickly than with the Imperial Government.

But when the settlers talk of the Chartered Company they really mean Mr. Rhodes. A Chartered Company without Mr. Rhodes, and really conducted by a Board in London, would probably be as distasteful to the colonists as the Imperial Government itself. But Mr. Rhodes is felt to be the guiding influence in the control of the Company's affairs; and he is here amongst the settlers, and ready to be grumbled at and bullied by them, whenever they think they have a grievance. He has not always been popular amongst them, and he was suspected at one time of thinking a great deal more about Pretoria than about Rhodesia. But now he is known to have his soul devoted to the country named after him, and his power of furthering or retarding its welfare, and the welfare of the individuals in it, is felt to be unsurpassable. He is not the managing director of the Company; he is not the administrator of the country; he cannot move a single policeman or confer a single Government appointment. But he is the founder of the country; he is yet a director of the Chartered

Company; he is director of the railway companies upon which the whole future of the country depends; he has put hundreds of thousands of pounds of his own money into the country and brought millions of pounds of other people's, and he owns an immense amount of personal property in it. Simply as a private individual he, therefore, stands far more to the settler and to the development companies than the most efficient administrator ever could. And farmers, merchants, and mining directors know that the exertion of his influence in the introduction of capital into the country and the pushing on of railway construction means so much more hard cash in their pockets. They, therefore, fully appreciate the benefit the country derives from his presence in it and his immense personal liberality towards them.

Yet these settlers do not look to continuing permanently the present despotic system of government. They are nearly all British, and consequently liberty-loving; and as soon as there is sufficient population they hope to see a self-governing colony, like the Cape or Natal, formed, when they can direct their own affairs. Rule by Chartered Company they prefer to direct administration by the Imperial Government; but they eventually hope to rule themselves, and form themselves into one more of our great self-governing colonies.

In the meantime the situation is delicate and difficult. The Imperial Government does not rule directly, but it exercises control; and the armed forces of the country, though paid for by the Company, are under the command of Imperial officers directly responsible to the Imperial Government. If a native chief is refractory, the Company's administration cannot move a single man to bring him to order. The Imperial Deputy Commissioner may consider the safety of the country requires that 1,000 men should be permanently entertained. The commercial Company, who have to pay for the men, would rather do with less. Friction must occur between the two authorities under this system. But the settlers may have the satisfaction of knowing that under it their safety is considered independently of the cost of protection; and, if this is not much consolation to the shareholders, it is at any rate for the good of the country. Men who know that they are only carrying on for a few years, and who are aware that in the event of trouble they can, by the despatch of a telegram to Cape Town, get up as many Imperial troops as they choose to ask for, at the rate of a shilling a day per man, may be suspected of a certain inclination to run risks, rather than pay 5s. a day per man for a permanent police force of adequate strength. The risk run is small; the saving considerable. But British taxpayers and British investors have also an interest in the matter. Without the support of the Imperial power, without that reserve of Imperial strength to fall back upon, the country could not stand. With the Germans on one side, the Boers on another, the Portuguese on a third, and the Belgians on the fourth, and with the interior full of hostile blacks, the country might stand for a time without Imperial support, but few people would feel inclined to invest their money in it; and it is upon the steady inflow of capital from Europe that the country is absolutely dependent for its prosperity. Gold mining in Rhodesia is sufficiently speculative as it is. The country could not afford to make it still more so. The settlers have, therefore, everything to gain from the Imperial Government's continuing to have its voice in the establishing of an adequate police force.

But, apart from the somewhat difficult position in which the Company are placed with regard to the control of their forces, they have constant difficulty as regards the *personnel* of their administration. South Africa, altogether, is badly off for recruits for the Civil Service. And the Chartered Company, in particular, have difficulties in obtaining efficient men, because they can offer no inducements of permanent service for life. The majority of their servants are men who take up employment for a few years while they can look about for more lucrative employment with mining companies. All are, more or less, engaged in speculation, and none of them can look to any higher appointment as a goal of ambition. There is no inducement, therefore, for first-class men to enter the Company's Civil Service, and the evil effects of the want of efficient men are especially felt in the native department.

To deal with natives men of the highest class are required, for the tendency to degenerate down to the level of the natives can be resisted only by the best. But the Company have hitherto used not the best class of men who come into the country, but almost the worst. A knowledge of the language was considered the primary essential. The field of choice was consequently limited, and the men who had the qualification were mostly small traders with little education, and quite unsuited to be put in positions of authority over men of a subject race. The result has been disastrous. But this defect the Company are now doing their best to remedy by introducing men from Natal who know the Zulu language (which is, practically, the same as the Matabele), and have had experience in native administration. And very careful attention is being paid to the whole system of controlling the natives.

Lord Grey's task, in the circumstances described above, is not an easy one. He succeeds a man who, for the work of starting a new colony, was unequalled, but who had not yet established the administration as a working machine. That has fallen to Lord Grey to accomplish. The rough-and-ready methods, the system of liberal grants and still more liberal promises, suitable for the first years of a colony, must now give place to more regular methods as the population increases. One of the most able men in the Cape Colonial Service—Mr. Milton—has been engaged by the Company to assist Lord Grey in the work of establishing departmental responsibility and putting the parts of the machine in true running order; and with the present influx of better men into the country, and with the experience of the past to guide them, there is every hope that this work will be satisfactorily accomplished.

CHAPTER XIV

INDIAN IMMIGRATION TO NATAL

Circumstances have forced Natal—one of the smallest and youngest but yet most interesting and progressive of all our colonies—to first tackle a question which, in coming years, must profoundly affect the whole British Empire. She lies comparatively close to the densely populated countries of India; she has a climate well suited to the inhabitants of India; and her colonists have found these Indians eminently useful in developing their agricultural districts, and have, therefore, not only encouraged but even assisted the immigration of Indian agriculturists to Natal. But the little stream which they were at first so anxious to direct into the colony has now swelled into a rushing river. The resources of the reservoir which has been tapped are practically illimitable, and if the swelling stream were not checked in some way the colony might soon be submerged in the dusky waters. And as with Natal so also may it be with the rest of the tropical and semi-tropical British colonies. India has a population which now numbers nearly three hundred millions, and this population is increasing at the rate of nearly three millions per annum. The means of communication between India and the colonies are, year by year, being made easier. Every year the natives of India are becoming better acquainted with lands beyond the seas. Every year more of them are being tempted to seek their fortunes in new countries; till, at the present time, Indian pedlars, Indian trading firms, and even Indian owners of steamship lines are found in the various countries bordering on the Indian Ocean.

South Africa is just become nervously aware of what this means to her. And though it is only in Natal that matters have yet come to a head, in all parts of South Africa I heard the question warmly discussed and the attitude of the Natalians eagerly watched. Natal is blamed by the other South African colonies for having encouraged so dangerous an immigration, and her new attitude in attempting to check it is thoroughly approved of. For the question is both a racial and a labour question. It is racial, not in the sense of their being any real symptoms of race hatred, but because the Anglo-Saxon colonists in South Africa are bent upon building up an Anglo-Saxon country, and believe that with a constant stream of immigrants from Great Britain they will be able to carry out their object if another stream from India is not allowed to mingle with it, to prevent that unity which can only come from similarity of social customs and ideas. And it is a labour question because the small British traders and the British artisans fear the competition of men accustomed to live more cheaply than they and be satisfied with less wages. Alike in the Transvaal, in Rhodesia and in the Free State I heard the opinions expressed that if South Africa was to be preserved "a white man's country," Indian immigration must be checked; and on my arrival in Natal I found the people who held the entrance ways by which the immigrants come in fully determined to carry out this object.

In January demonstrations on a large scale had been made at Durban to prevent the landing of two ship loads of Indians who had come from Bombay. Two or three thousand men had assembled on the quays, and expressed their intention of forcibly ejecting any Indian who attempted to put his foot on shore. A good deal of over-violent language was used by the leaders of the agitation, and a nasty crisis was only averted by the tact of Mr. Escombe, the then Attorney-General, who, in an address to the crowd, threw the responsibility of any bloodshed which might occur upon the leaders of the agitation, yet at the same time promised that Government would in the present Session bring in measures to deal with the question. But though the words and actions of the extreme agitators were disapproved of by the majority of men I met, I was left in no doubt that even the most moderate of the colonists desired that the Indian immigration should be checked. These men do not attempt to hide the value of the Indian to the colony in a variety of ways; for they allow that a great deal of the prosperity of the colony is due to the influx of Indian labour on the sugar, tea, and fruit estates. And they say that if only agriculturists came from India they would make no complaint. White men cannot work in the fields in Natal, and therefore Indians who work with a greater degree of intelligence than the Kaffirs would be welcome. But the immigration of Indians is not confined to the agricultural classes only. Swarms of petty traders have also come in and entirely ousted the class of small white traders who used formerly to find a living in the colony. Larger Indian traders are acquiring property in the principal towns, and conducting considerable establishments. Indian artisans are competing with European artisans, and gradually driving them out of the field.

Theoretically it may be argued that such competition must in the main be of advantage to the colony, that it will reduce the price of commodities to the consumer and the price of labour to the employer. And in practice many of the colonists follow out the theory; for the farmer's wife, if she can get her necessaries cheaper from an Indian store than she can from a European store, will go to the Indian; and many of the agitators employed Indians largely where Europeans might have been used if they could have been had for equally low wages. Yet, in spite of this inconsistency, they would prefer to see the country rid of Indian traders and artisans; and this deep underlying feeling which prevails among the colonists was made especially clear to me by the past and present Mayors of Durban, Mr. Jameson and Mr. Payne, who took me round the town and showed the immense progress which had been made by the British settlers, and explained how they wished to hand the colony down to their children a British colony and not a semi-Asiatic country like Mauritius. They argued that they and their fathers had fought for it and formed the foundation of its prosperity. I was shown when forty years ago only a few rough houses formed the nucleus of the present town of Durban, and from the clock-tower of the present Town Hall was pointed out how the town had grown to its present size, street after street being formed, and shops, business houses and hotels springing up on every side. I was then taken to the line of quays, and shown the immense improvements which had there been made till Durban has become one of the first ports in South Africa. And the question which presented itself to me was, "Would all this have been accomplished if the proportion of Indians to Europeans had been greater? Allowing that Indians have a large amount of enterprise and commercial ability, have they the initiative and energy to push a young colony?" The colonists believe they have not. They believe that with every Indian trader who takes up a position which might have been filled by a European, there is a loss of that impulsive force which a young colony requires. The Indian is separate from the European settler in religion, customs, ideas and principles. There is no possibility of his amalgamating with the original British and Dutch settlers, as Germans, French or Russians would. The two will always remain separate. Moreover the Indian is passive not active. He has none of that *idée du corps* of a European settler; none of that feeling that he is part of a colony, and that, apart from his own interests, he must push the interests of the colony as a whole, that indeed his own interests are inseparably wrapt up in the interests of the whole community. This is what the colonists feel about the Indians, and this is what is at the root of their opposition to them. Germans, French or any other European nationality may come as many as they please, and they are welcome, because they settle down, they intermarry, they become part and parcel of the community interested in its welfare and ready to further its progress. But the Indians the colonists regard as a blight upon the colony, as doing no active harm, but as occupying places which, but for their presence, might have been occupied by others who would have become active powers for good in the development of the colony.

And what of the Indian side of the question? Undoubtedly, to the Indian Natal is a perfect paradise. The climate is exactly suited to him, neither too hot nor too cold; and he obtains there wages for his labour and profits on his business enterprises which he would never obtain in his own country. At the same time he is under a strong government, which protects him in a way he never would be in any Asiatic country. He has his grievances, and of those I was made acquainted by Mr. Gandhi, the leading merchant of Durban. But I think these are not so much grievances at their present as at their prospective treatment. Mr. Gandhi, the spokesman of the Indian community and the butt of the agitators, is a particularly intelligent and well-educated man, who has studied for three years in England and lives in a well-furnished English villa at Durban. At a dinner, to which he and the leading Indians invited me, I found merchants who had visited England and several other countries in Europe, who had bought steamers in Glasgow and conducted business on a large scale, and who could talk fluently in English on all the current events of the time. Such men as these naturally resent the use of the term "coolie," which is indiscriminately applied to high and low class Indians by the colonists. And they complain of the objections which are frequently made to their travelling in upper class compartments in the trains and tramcars. But while they complain of being classed separately from Europeans, they are much offended at Kafirs being classed with them. And, on the whole, in spite of occasional rudeness from rough colonists, I do not think that the Indians in Natal are badly treated personally, and compensation for injuries can always be obtained in the law courts, where the astute Indian is well able to look after his interests.

What, however, they undoubtedly have to feel anxious about is their future treatment. As Mr. Gandhi pointed out to me, the restrictions placed upon them are being increased year by year, and they feel that they must protest against each, not so much because any single restriction placed upon them so far has been too unbearable, but because these restrictions are now accumulating to a degree when they might be, and they think that without protest they may be, piled up still more heavily. Originally they had the franchise in full. Now this is restricted, and a poll tax is levied on Indians who at the close of their term of indenture elect to remain in the colony. Finally, the Natal Government this year brought in measures which, though they are not ostensibly directed against Asiatics, were undoubtedly intended to check their immigration. In deference to the wishes of the Imperial Government no mention was made of class or colour, but Town Councils were given the power to refuse the grant of annual trading licences to persons not keeping their books in English, or dwelling in premises not fit for the intended trade, or provided with proper sanitary arrangements; and the immigration laws were so amended that any person who was unable to write out and sign in the characters of any language of Europe a particular application form, or any person who was not possessed of available means of subsistence of his own to the value of £25, might be refused admission to the colony.

This is how the colony of Natal has attempted to deal with the difficult and delicate question brought upon it. The Indians lay claim to completeness of liberty upon their status as British subjects; and to put restriction on British subjects in a British colony is an anomalous attitude. But the law of self-preservation is the first law of being; and when we find young men in England advised against going to Natal and other parts of South Africa because the position they might otherwise have taken up is now occupied by Indians, we need not be surprised that the colonists are so determined to restrict the immigration that they affirm that if the price of Empire is that they must necessarily allow every Indian exactly the same privileges that would be granted to a native of Great Britain, then they would prefer to be independent of the Empire and be free to work out their career by themselves. And Indians have no great right to complain even if immigration is restricted; for during all the centuries of the past they might have done with Natal what British colonists with courage and enterprise and resource now have accomplished. It can therefore be no special hardship or injustice to them if the colonists allow them to eat of the fruit of their labours in limited quantities and refuse to permit them to bear down the whole tree.

CHAPTER XV

THE OUTLOOK IN SOUTH AFRICA

In this final chapter it will be useful to summarise the various impressions I formed during my stay of twelve months in South Africa. In my two visits to the country I not only saw it at its most interesting crisis, but in addition to a sojourn of six months in the Transvaal I traversed the length of Rhodesia and I travelled through the Cape Colony, the native territories, Natal and the Portuguese possessions round Delagoa Bay.

As a seething mass of unassimilated elements it would be hard to equal the South Africa that I saw. From the Zambesi to Cape Colony there was unrest. Nowhere did there appear coherency, unity, or security, and what chance there was of the various antagonistic elements slowly settling down had been incalculably thrown back by the raid, the full results of which are only now being duly realised.

The British settlers believe the preposterously heavy arming of the Boers means that they intend to assume the offensive. The Transvaal suspects that an attack may again be made upon it; for the Boers, and especially their President, regard Mr. Rhodes as their implacable enemy. They believe that the British people and British Government in heart support him; and they require no pressing to obey Mr. Kruger's recently-expressed injunction to "prepare for war."

The sister Dutch Republic of the Orange Free State would like to hold aloof from any disturbances, but feels that this may be impossible. It fears that, if the Transvaal lost its independence, its own independence would soon go likewise. So the Free State joins with the Transvaal in its preparation for war.

Whatever tends towards a conflict between the Dutch and the British in the Republics tends to division in the Cape Colony and Natal, with their white population half British and half Dutch; and in the former colony especially there is a marked accentuation of that racial feeling which for some years yet must inevitably exist. The Cape Dutch sympathised with the Uitlanders in their grievances, but the supposed attack upon the independence of the Transvaal roused all their national sympathy with men of their own blood; and the feeling amongst perhaps the majority of them is that, if any unprovoked attack were now made, they would have to join their compatriots in a struggle against British interference.

Again, dissension between the two great divisions

of the white population of South Africa necessarily tends to cause unrest among the more numerous black population held in subjection by the whites. And the restless feeling engendered among the natives by the divisions between the Dutch and English has been increased by the appearance of that terrible disease which is cutting off the one great source of wealth to the blacks. So that on leaving Rhodesia, where rebellion had only just been stamped out, at the first town in the Cape Colony I entered I found the people hastily rushing to arms in expectation of a native rising, and a punitive expedition had to be sent against the chiefs who rose in rebellion. Travelling on to East Griqualand I found a similar scare had occurred there also, and the farmers in several districts had collected together into laager. In Basutoland I found a crisis had only been averted by the tact and decision of Mr. Lagden, the Resident.

The tension was, then, on all sides so great that any display of temper by either party would have set South Africa in a blaze. Each one was asking, "When is this state of things to end? How is confidence again to be restored?"

Before attempting to offer any solution of this question I must briefly review the main factors in the situation. Of the two white races of South Africa one is backward and slow in movement, while the other is essentially progressive. Over the greater part of South Africa the progressive section is in power; but the richest portion of the country is held by the unprogressive section. And the development of the whole of South Africa depending so much as it does upon the development of the Transvaal, the pushing, energetic section are kept in a state of constant irritation at the deliberateness of the more backward section, while these latter are ever in a nervous dread that the progressives may filch their portion from them. The feeling of the British throughout South Africa towards the Dutch of the Transvaal is, "Move along, or let us manage affairs." And the feeling of the Transvaal Dutch towards the British is, "Push ahead as much as you like in your own part of South Africa, but leave us alone in ours." If the Boers had Bechuanaland instead of the Transvaal, or if the Transvaal were as devoid of mineral wealth as is the Free State, there would be no more tension between the Dutch and English than there was between the two in the Free State before the raid. The disturbing factor in the situation is the wealth of the Transvaal.

Of this wealth there is, we have already seen, absolutely no doubt. Much of it will be wasted through the incompetence of the Government; for mines which would pay well if a sympathetic Government were in power to facilitate the development of the industry, are now turning out gold at a loss. But in all parts of the Transvaal, as well as on the Rand, gold is to be found. And, besides the gold, there is a practically unlimited quantity of both coal and iron, while, in addition, the country has a good soil and enjoys a healthy climate.

The thousands of men and women flocking to South Africa from every part of crowded Europe in search of a livelihood are now beginning to ask whether all this wealth can be allowed to run to waste, whether the Boers are justified in keeping so rigorously in their own hands a country which, if properly administered, might afford a home and comfortable living to hundreds of thousands of the over-populated States of Europe, and whether they are really following out the precepts of their often-quoted Bible when they persist in wrapping up their talent in a napkin and making nothing further of it.

The Boers, for their part, recognising the wealth of their country — though only partially, for they cling to the idea that gold is the sole source of wealth, and that even that will last but a small number of years—fear this flood of strangers pouring into the Transvaal, and suspect these aliens of a desire to appropriate the country to themselves. They have seen their country once already annexed by the British. They last year had to resist a determined effort to subvert their authority. And they have this year seen indications which, rightly or wrongly, lead them to believe that that effort may again be renewed. The instinct of self-preservation—the most powerful and pressing instinct which can affect a nation—induces them to adopt an attitude of armed defence. They will fight for their independence to the last. They will not, unless absolutely compelled by force, allow strangers any share in the control of the country. And, further, there has been recent indications of a policy to discourage immigration, to make matters so uncomfortable that aliens will have no wish to settle in the country. To prepare themselves against an open invasion by an armed defence, and to check a slow, insidious invasion by measures of restraint—this seems to be the policy which the instinct of self-preservation is dictating to the Boers.

And, such being their attitude, there are many Englishmen in South Africa who say that the only hope for a settlement of differences and for a restoration of confidence in business is for Great Britain to "have it out" with the Transvaal, to insist by force that British subjects should be treated as liberally in the Transvaal as the Dutch are in Cape Colony, and to make the Boers of the Transvaal really subservient to the British. And, in their opinion, the sooner this is done the better, for the longer the blow is delayed the more fully armed will the Boers be. There will be no peace or feeling of security, they argue, till this is done. "Do something, whether right or wrong, but at any rate act," is what they say, "and get a decision one way or another, so that we may know where we are in future."

That Great Britain has the power to act in this way is undeniable. The Transvaal is nearly surrounded by British territory, and its frontier may be crossed at almost any point. The British have incalculably greater wealth and larger numbers of men for the prosecution of a war. And those who have money invested in the country would be only too pleased if British taxpayers would furnish the twenty millions of money and send out the thirty thousand men required to subjugate the Transvaal, and, by substituting a liberal and progressive Government for the obstructive government of Dutch farmers, enhance the value of their properties.

Others, however, and among them those who have lived longest in South Africa, ask, "Would it be possible to confine such a conflict to the Transvaal, or would it not rather spread throughout South Africa? Might it not affect the relations between blacks and whites also, and bring murdering hordes of savages upon defenceless farms and villages throughout the country? And what is to be the result of the war? Will racial feeling—Dutch and English, black and white—be diminished or increased thereby? Will the stubborn Dutchmen, who have struggled for their independence for centuries, suddenly give up their aspirations and submit like lambs; or would it not be necessary rather to keep up a strong permanent garrison in

South Africa to retain them in a state of subjugation and prevent the risk of constantly-recurring efforts to regain their independence?"

These are the questions asked by men who demand further what advantage has ever been gained in South Africa by hurry. Undue haste, they point out, has been the cause of every one of the South African mistakes and disasters from our shortsighted act in withdrawing from the Free State, forty years ago, the sovereignty they begged us to retain over them, to our premature attempt at confederation in 1877, our annexation of the Transvaal, and lastly the Jameson raid. Each one of these acts, instead of rendering South African unity more certain, has made it more remote, has tended to consolidate the Dutch Republics against us, has prevailed and intensified the national feeling among them.

The Boers have few of the characteristics required for the formation of a coherent nation, and the wide vastnesses of the countries they occupy serve only to increase their tendency to disintegrate. Their impatience of restraint, their unwillingness to submit to the irksomeness of government are proverbial. When left alone they have always shown a tendency to division; and the present struggle between the judicial body on the one hand and the legislative and executive bodies on the other is the latest example of the incapacity of a people of low social development to form a united nation without pressure from outside to keep them together.

But it is precisely this necessary pressure that the British have always been so ready to give them; and it is the British alone whom the Boers have to thank for causing their preservation as a separate nation. One of the leading statesmen in the Dutch Republics was perfectly right when he told me that it was only the constant succession of acts of British interference that had fostered and increased the spirit of Republicanism among the Dutch in opposition to British Imperial control, and that if they had been left alone there would have now been none of that combined antagonism to the British which unfortunately at present exists.

And as long as they suspect that the British have designs upon the Transvaal, that they covet its riches, and are only watching for an opportunity of destroying its independence, the sympathies of the Cape Dutch will be with the Transvaal Boers. But this undercurrent of distrust which pervades the Cape Dutch to-day has not always been there. On the contrary, for some years past up to the time of the raid the tendency was towards a gradual abatement of that strong clannish feeling among the Dutch against the British. While many even among the prominent Dutch had formerly dreamed of, and perhaps worked for, the establishment of a Dutch Republic throughout South Africa with

British supremacy dwindled down to a control of coaling stations only, those hopes were gradually disappearing under the liberal form of government to which they were subjected. At the same time there was a feeling among them against the Transvaal Boers because of the seclusive and obstructive policy which shut up the country not only against the rush of immigrants from Europe, but even against their fellow-countrymen in South Africa. A Cape Dutch Afrikander—even a Dutch Afrikander of the Free State—was excluded from the rights of citizenship in the Transvaal just as rigorously as the rest of the Uitlanders. Their produce was as heavily taxed; and, most cruel of all, Dutchmen from Holland were imported for service in the Government offices in the Transvaal, when Dutch Afrikanders had apparently all the necessary qualifications of language and education and compatriotism, and sorely needed employment.

What, then, is offered as a solution of the problem as an alternative to the employment of force? One solution suggested is the extreme opposite policy—the leaving matters absolutely alone, and submitting to arbitration any questions in dispute between the Transvaal and Great Britain. Such a course of inaction has, however, few advocates. It would mean the abnegation by Great Britain of the claims she has always made to be considered the paramount Power in South Africa;

it would encourage the Boers in that policy of passive obstruction to which they are by nature so fatally addicted; and it would involve the indefinite postponement of that general development of South Africa which the British race have so energetically undertaken. The Transvaal has treaty obligations with England which her policy of recent years gives England no inducement to abrogate. And the common belief is that those obligations are more likely to be carried out if the Transvaal feels that the paramount Power in South Africa is prepared at any moment to enforce them than if the points were submitted to the slow uncertain process of arbitration.

But the obligations are not all on one side. England is under obligations to the Transvaal as the Transvaal is to England, and has undertaken to respect the internal independence of the country. Viewing, then, the South African question as a whole; regarding the development of the country as a settlement for European races to be the primary object in view; looking upon that development of the whole country to be mainly dependent on the development of the richest part—the Transvaal; and recognising that racial differences—Dutch and English, black and white—immensely retard that development, the wisest policy which suggests itself for England to pursue seems to be that of abstention from any direct interference in the internal affairs of the Transvaal, while at the same time maintaining in the strictest manner the rights of free access of her subjects to the country and of just treatment while in it which the London Convention confers; and, further, bringing again into sympathy with her all that body of Dutch opinion in the Cape Colony, Natal, and the Free State which has been estranged by recent events.

When this weight of Dutch colonial feeling, upon which the Transvaal Boers at present confidently count, can be transferred again to the British side in furtherance of a policy which will open up the Transvaal to Afrikanders of every part of South Africa; and when Continental opinion can be made to realise the advantages which are to be gained by supporting, instead of thwarting, Great Britain in her work of developing South Africa; the 70,000 Boers who now bar the way to progress must inevitably give way, and the development of the Transvaal, upon which depends so much of the prosperity of South Africa, be definitely assured.

INDEX